Albie Sachs and Transformation in South Africa

Many critical theorists talk and write about the day after the revolution, but few have actually participated in the constitution of a revolutionary government. Emeritus Justice Albie Sachs was a freedom fighter for most of his life. He then played a major role in the negotiating committee for the new constitution of South Africa, and was subsequently appointed to the new Constitutional Court of South Africa. Therefore, the question of what it means to make the transition from a freedom fighter to a participant in a revolutionary government is not abstract, in Hegel's sense of the word: it is an actual journey undertaken by Albie Sachs.

The essays in this book raise the complex question of what it actually means to make this transition without selling out to the demands of realism. In addition, the preface written by Emeritus Justice Albie Sachs, and his interview with Drucilla Cornell and Karin van Marle, further address key questions about revolution in the twentieth and twenty-first centuries: from armed struggle to the organization of a nation state committed to ethical transformation in the name of justice.

Albie Sachs and Transformation in South Africa: From Revolutionary Activist to Constitutional Court Judge illuminates the theoretical and practical experiences of revolution and its political aftermath. With first-hand accounts alongside academic interrogation, this unique book will intrigue anyone interested in the intersection of law and politics.

Drucilla Cornell is Professor of Political Science, Women Studies, and Comparative Literature at Rutgers University (New Brunswick), a visiting professor at Birkbeck College in London and a Professor Extraordinaire at the University of Pretoria in South Africa.

Karin van Marle is Professor and Head of the Department of Jurisprudence at the University of Pretoria. She works from an ethical feminist perspective and situates post-apartheid jurisprudence within the field of law, culture, and the humanities.

Albie Sachs is Emeritus Justice of the Constitutional Court of South Africa. Previous to this appointment, he was a freedom fighter in South Africa and subsequently played a major role in the negotiating committee for the new constitution of South Africa.

Albie Sachs and Transformation in South Africa

From Revolutionary Activist to Constitutional Court Judge

Drucilla Cornell and
Karin van Marle,
with Albie Sachs

Birkbeck
LAW PRESS

First published 2014
by Birkbeck Law Press
2 Park Square, Milton Park, Abingdon, Oxon, OX14 4RN

and by Birkbeck Law Press
711 Third Avenue, New York, NY 10017

Birkbeck Law Press is an imprint of the Taylor & Francis Group, an informa business

British Library Cataloguing in Publication Data
A catalogue record for this book is available from the British Library

Library of Congress Cataloging-in-Publication Data
Cornell, Drucilla, author.
Albie Sachs and transformation in South Africa : from revolutionary activist to constitutional court judge / Drucilla Cornell and Karin van Marle with Albie Sachs.
pages cm
1. Sachs, Albie, 1935- 2. Judges—South Africa—Biography.
3. Lawyers—South Africa—Biography. I. Van Marle, Karin, author.
II. Title.
KTL110.S23C67 2014
342.6802'69092—dc23
2013033374

ISBN: 978-0-415-73516-2 (hbk)

ISBN: 978-1-315-81934-1 (ebk)

Typeset in Garamond 3 by
Florence Production Ltd, Stoodleigh, Devon

Contents

Acknowledgements vii
Preface ix

Introduction 1
DRUCILLA CORNELL AND KARIN VAN MARLE

1 Comrade judge: can a revolutionary be a judge? 9
DRUCILLA CORNELL

2 Abandoning certitudes, becoming human — for a jurisprudence of generosity: an essay in tribute to the work of Albie Sachs 49
KARIN VAN MARLE

3 Interview with Emeritus Justice Albie Sachs 75
DRUCILLA CORNELL AND KARIN VAN MARLE

Notes 115
Index 125

to Sarita, Hannah and Oliver

for the hope they inspire.

Acknowledgements

We want to thank Emeritus Justice Albie Sachs for his participation in this book. It has been an honor and a privilege to work with him. His integrity and courage as a revolutionary and then as a justice inspired us to tackle this project which turned out to be more than a critical engagement with his jurisprudence. His life, writings, and judgements engage some of the most pressing issues of our time as we enter an age of political resistance.

We also want to thank Costas Douzinas. Costas Douzinas has been a friend and supporter of both of us over so many years. His enthusiasm for this book helped us to bring it to fruition.

The two anonymous reviewers gave us insightful comments and helped us in the last stages of writing. We are in their debt.

We dedicate this book to our children. Sarita, Hannah and Oliver.

Preface

I don't know who was more surprised, the Vice-President of the Supreme Court of the People's Republic of China or my colleagues on the Constitutional Court of the newly democratic South Africa. At a rather solemn meeting, I had suddenly started singing in a soft voice. "Arise, you who refuse to be bondslaves, let's stand up and fight for liberty and true democracy . . . Chi lai . . ." I was taking a chance, trusting that I could later explain I'd learnt the words 50 years earlier as a young law student in a movement dreaming of a revolutionary overthrow of apartheid and transformation of the world, and that we had sung along with a recording by Paul Robeson, the great African-American singer and freedom fighter. But at that moment, we were facing each other at a judicial gathering underneath a giant mobile of hand-carved birds in our Court's vibrant meeting room, and there was no going back. "All of us are breaking the chains of the tyrants, arise, arise . . ." And, to my relief, the Vice-President and his entourage began to relax their stern, formal expressions and started to smile, at first tentatively, then more warmly before finally breaking into huge appreciative grins — they'd realized I was singing the English version of the Chinese National Anthem! And, I should mention, when to this day I continue to sing along quietly when the anthem is played as the Chinese flag is raised at international sporting events, I do so not so much to pay tribute to the excellence of the athletes, as to honor the idealism of my youth, and wonder wryly how much of it has survived my change of station.

The fact is that the person who had once dreamt of becoming a great revolutionary had now become the great legitimizer. From attending clandestine meetings in parked cars with the lights off, or under a tree on the mountainside as the rain fell down, and plotting the overthrow of the state, I had moved to sitting publicly in robes with 10 colleagues on the highest court in the land, laying down the law for the whole of my society.

Looking back, I can see that, as in so many other things, art had anticipated change before history had brought it about: as I never tire of saying, our jazz musicians wrote our Constitution in music long before we lawyers wrote it in law. But this time it was theatre that did the pre-figuring for me . . . a friend was in a play he thought might be of interest; its title wasn't very promising, and it was by an unknown German writer, but I might enjoy seeing a piece about a revolutionary who becomes a judge. And so I spent a great evening in a little university theatre puzzled and enthralled by the manner in which a comrade judge solved the problem of the village: who should get custody of a baby . . . the cold and remote upper-class mother who had borne the child and had every claim to it in law, or the child's nursemaid, a peasant woman who had cared for and loved it since birth, and whose claim to entitlement was simply that she had done all the actual mothering? The comrade judge's solution was to draw a circle on the stage and tell each woman to take an arm and a leg and pull . . . the one who showed the strength to pull the baby out of the circle would obviously be the one who wanted the baby the most, and therefore be the one to keep the child. Readers who have seen "The Caucasian Chalk Circle" by Bertold Brecht will know that the nursemaid let go of the baby, preferring to relinquish her claim rather than see it get hurt, proving to the comrade judge that she would be the better mother. And so it was decided that she was entitled under the new revolutionary law to keep the baby.

And years later, when I was locked up in solitary confinement, left with my clothes and nothing else except a Bible, I came to read the same story in the Book of Solomon. I was rationing myself to a few pages a day, and after being severely distressed by what I felt to be the harsh zealotry and implacable inwardness of much of the Old Testament, and before being exalted by the majestic vision of peace and freedom for all humanity projected by the prophets, I got special delight from poring over the poetic and gentle section on Solomon. The songs were beautiful, and Solomon's outreach to all people, especially those in Africa, was wonderful. But above all, he was not just another astute ruler filled with zeal to smite enemies: he was a cultivated and wise person, imbued with humanity. Was he in fact, I wondered, the first great revolutionary judge? After all, when he famously tested the two women who each claimed the child, by offering to cut the infant in half, and then awarded it to the one who preferred to give up her half rather than see the child injured, did he not put humane concern and respect for human dignity above formal lineage and succession rights?

But much as I loved and mused over these tales, neither Brecht nor the Bible prompted me to imagine that one day I would find myself cast in the role of a judge in a country undergoing major transformation. Nor did I dream of having to reflect upon the extent to which the revolutionary idealism which was inspiring me in the underground in that, the first part of my life, would connect up with my work on the court in this, the second.

And that is the organizing theme of this unusual book: during the years when I had been transformed from defiant poacher challenging state authority, into established gamekeeper protecting the realm, what, if anything, had survived of my revolutionary dreams?

I guess every intellectual likes to be taken seriously, even if preferably not by imprisonment or assassination. I certainly take seriously being taken seriously, especially if pushed by two brainy and intrepid interlocutors into new zones of thought where I feel slightly out of my depth. So I responded readily to the question put to me, realizing that, disconcerting though it might be for me personally, it had a relevance that went far beyond my particular situation. The world is full of former rebels who have ended up in old or new establishments. Using his artistic imagination, Carlos Fuentes explored this theme beautifully in *The Life and Death of Artemio Cruz*. But whereas Fuentes dealt primarily with deeds and ruptures in his sardonic study, this book focuses in a slightly more hopeful way on values and continuities.

And if the reader is curious about the context in which the continuity or otherwise of values was evidenced while I was on the Bench, the following information might be of interest.

In terms of physical appearance, the outward signs of the one-time revolutionary idealist were there for all to see. When I'd been blown up by a bomb put in my car by apartheid operatives and lost an arm, a comrade from my youth movement days had written to say I would cut a romantic figure. I enjoyed the description! Equally, I was delighted when an African comrade had told me shortly after the bomb that the enemy had Africanized me by giving me scars on my face like Oliver Tambo. To complete the picture, as a tiny act of rebellion against the wearing of boring suits, I would put on art ties when I went to work . . . Michelangelo, Picasso, Magritte, Klee, Van Gogh, Monet, Dali, and many more.

Then, the new court to which I belonged immediately revolutionized judicial style. There were lots of little things: we dropped the titles My Lord and My Lady, and asked not to be called Honorable; many of us chose to use Hondas or Toyotas rather than take the BMWs and Mercedes offered to us by the Department of Justice; we cut out the use of Latin in our judgments; and shocked some in the Department when we said that rather than take up valuable space for toilets in each of our Chambers, we would share ablutions with the rest of the staff. Small details, perhaps, but all indicative of a new mentality. And the more hierarchical a setting, the greater the impact that change of detail has. Perhaps more important was the way in which we workshopped ideas before writing our judgments, going round and round the table many times, convening and re-convening in pursuit of better understanding of the issues. And although the Chief and Deputy Chief Justice had fixed positions on the Bench to enable them to preside, the rest of us moved our seating every term to underline the fact that there was no hierarchy based on seniority in our court. These were changes agreed to collectively. We came from many philosophical backgrounds, with different life experiences, but I suspect that what united us in respect of transforming these minutiae of court functioning was our eagerness to get away from the institutional pomposity and formalism that had masked the substantive injustices of the past.

Then we revolutionized the architectural aesthetic of court buildings. Thus, our building had totally new features: it had been constructed in the heart of the Old Fort Prison, where both Gandhi and Mandela had been locked up; prison cells abutted the Court, while an original prison staircase still stood in the foyer; the Court Chamber was clad with bricks from demolished parts of the prison, while the Bench on which we judges sat was only slightly raised, so that our eyes were at the same level as the eyes of counsel addressing us; the doors, carpets, security gates, and lamps of the building had all been designed by artists who had won public competitions; the building was filled with artwork made by famous artists as well as by barely known crafters from rural communities; and, above all, the building was light and friendly, reflecting the principle of justice under a tree, welcoming to all and sundry, and especially to those who historically had been frightened to enter massive buildings that projected themselves as representing the power of the state or the dominion of the wealthy (unless, of course, they sneaked in through back entrances to clean and guard the building).

Constitution Hill, as the area is now called, is a physical link between three worlds normally kept apart: a densely populated and poor part of the city to the east, leafy suburbs to the north, and the bureaucratic hub to the west and south. In short, the building was not built as a monument to the freedom struggle: it was designed to be a continuing part of the freedom struggle, and to epitomize in its very openness and sense of humaneness the values of human dignity, equality, and freedom that lay at the core of the constitutional endeavor. And I would not deny it if somebody said a relevant fact might have been that shortly after the Court was established, the Chief Justice appointed Yvonne Mokgoro and myself to be responsible for décor.

But, as the saying goes, you shouldn't judge a book by its cover. Indeed, rainbowism has become something of a term of abuse in South Africa, allegedly representing a pretty and soft-centered sentimentality that hides harsh realities of division and conflict. What mattered the most in terms of assessing continuity of idealism, then, was not the outward show of change, but the intrinsic character of the value system incorporated into the Court's judgments. Was there any connection between the revolutionary spirit possessed by the young Albie and the spirit of the laws as upheld by the older one?

To answer this question, I ask another one. What was the most burning hope I had as a young lawyer and activist? To be a good revolutionary! But the problem was that I never found out what a good revolutionary was. The nearest I got was when, not long out of hospital, I refused to allow a top ANC official to push my trolley at Heathrow airport, and he turned admiringly to others in the group and said: comrade Albie is a true revolutionary! Fortunately, my interviewers didn't focus on questions of definition, but simply assumed that revolutionary idealism existed, and pushed me to reflect on the role it played in the armed struggle: was all fair in love, war, and revolution, could a liberation movement use torture to combat attempts to destroy it? And then, was there a connection between the underlying revolutionary idealism of that period and the constitutional idealism of my years on the Bench? In responding to their queries, I explained how my experience of living through the Mozambican Revolution for 11 years had persuaded me that the emancipatory ideas at the heart of my being could better be realized in an open, democratic, and pluralistic society than in one based on a post-revolutionary state monolithically defending the gains of the revolution. But the emancipatory impulse, I liked to feel, had not changed.

It will be up to you, the reader, to decide if positive or negative connections have been established between the two periods of idealistic endeavor, the first at the time of struggle and the second at the time of adjudicating. In doing so, you might ponder over a fact that has both energized and baffled me right through my life. It is that there is a contradiction at the heart of idealism — if it is not transcendent, it is not ideal; but if it transcends reality and experience, it is futile. You might like to think that one over.

Albie Sachs
Cape Town and Nairobi, September 2012

The Defiance Campaign

Source: Albie Sachs documentary collection at the Mayibuye Centre.

Introduction

Drucilla Cornell and Karin van Marle

Emeritus Justice Albie Sachs became a freedom fighter as a young law student at the University of Cape Town. Although he did not join the armed struggle, it was not because of ideological opposition, but because of an injured knee. For a good portion of his life, Sachs lived as an outlaw after enduring imprisonment and torture. He has ruefully noted that although he served the struggle against apartheid primarily as a writer, educator, and lawyer, the armed struggle caught up with him. He was literally blown up by a bomb placed in a car by the security agents of the South African Government, which cost him an arm and the sight in one eye. As he himself writes:

> The fact is that for much of my life I lived simultaneously as lawyer and as outlaw. Anyone who has been in clandestinity will know how split the psyche becomes when you work through the law in the public sphere, and against the law in the underground. Yet the causes were easy to understand and the resolution as obvious to predict — only when we ended apartheid and realigned the law with justice, could I become whole again.[1]

This book is about the jurisprudence of Albie Sachs as a Justice on the Constitutional Court of South Africa and about the complexity of the transformation that had to take place both politically and personally in Sachs's journey from revolutionary idealism through developing legal institutions as part of revolutionary struggle.[2] The dilemmas of the transition from freedom fighter to judge and the struggle to bring law closer to justice are what make Sachs's jurisprudential journey important to anyone concerned with the relation among revolution, justice, and law. His work with the Mozambique Liberation Front (*Frente de Libertação de Moçambique* — FRELIMO) brought him to the forefront of efforts to develop a revolutionary jurisprudence worthy of a constitution committed to social and economic transformation. As Sachs's experience in Mozambique shows us, the struggle to think through the meaning of revolutionary jurisprudence and a transformatory constitution worthy of the mandate to do justice is certainly not only a South African problem. We see in his jurisprudence a beckoning of a more general angle that asks law to give up exactly what makes it law, its certitude, and thereby exposing it to the possibility/experiment of becoming more human. His writings on and engagements with law could be read to stand in the guise of law giving up, or at least doubting certitude and becoming more human. The idea of post-apartheid law becoming human by giving up certitudes could be one attempt to bring about a substantive transformation that goes beyond a mere change in form and that could contribute to a broader notion of social reconciliation.[3] Sachs's contribution to post-apartheid jurisprudence through his judgments, but also beyond judgments his writings and reflections on judgment, has played a significant role in opening paths for a radical transformation that could be true to the substantive revolution that occurred. Post-apartheid jurisprudence, the jurisprudence in the aftermath of an authoritarian and violent past, cannot only be concerned with the consciousness or wisdom of law, but must also involve a deep and continuous exploration of law's conscience. Sachs's jurisprudence is witness to both of these.

The history of the struggle of South Africa has almost become symbolic of a freedom fight that did not end in defeat, but was capable of creating a new dispensation at a moment in which deep pessimism about transformation seemed pervasive in many countries of the world. This book has to be understood against the background of the prolonged and heroic struggle of the people of South Africa to end apartheid. Let us turn to a brief summary of that history as it relates to Sachs's trajectory as a fighter for human rights, social transformation, and justice for all.

In 1994, Nelson Mandela was elected president of the new Republic of South Africa. Mandela was one of the leaders of the African National Congress and of Umkhonto we Sizwe (Spear of the Nation), the underground army that was formed after many years of attempts to end racial oppression in South Africa peacefully. He was elected in the first popular vote that included the black majority population. Even cynical television commentators commented almost in awe on the long lines of voters often waiting for hours to cast the first vote of a lifetime. The spirit of those lines was joyous and exuberant. After being excluded from meaningful political rights for over a century, the majority population was now voting. It was a big victory indeed. Long viewed as a dangerous outlaw, Nelson Mandela was now elected president.

How did this victory come about? It has often been hailed as a miracle.[4] But it was not a miracle at all. The African National Congress (ANC) was founded in 1912, beginning its long struggle to end all forms of racial, economic, and political oppression. The struggle was terribly difficult. Many activists were banned, exiled, or imprisoned, as we have seen in the life of Albie Sachs; many endured the worst kind of torture. The ANC did everything it could to fight on for freedom with non-violent, peaceful means. But the brutality they faced made any kind of political protest impossible. Therefore, the mass movement finally came to the conclusion that the only way to end the horrifying oppression of the majority population was to engage in an armed struggle.[5]

In the talk of miracles, the everyday heroism of the people who participated in that struggle is often forgotten.[6] The struggle against apartheid became ever-more prominent after the Soweto uprising of 1976. On June 16, 1976, schoolchildren in Soweto attempted to deliver a petition asking that their courses no longer be conducted in Afrikaans, a language they considered to be the language of the oppressor. They never reached the city offices with their petition, because police opened fire. As is often the case in the twentieth century, one photograph pointed to the horror of that day. It was a photograph of Hector Peterson being carried by one of his comrades after being shot. From 1976 onwards, a series of mass movements challenged the ever-increasingly repressive government. Steven Biko, originally a student leader, formed the Black Consciousness movement, which inspired a generation of young people not only to take to the streets, but to assert a completely different notion of what it meant to be black against the racial epithets that were the slogans of the apartheid government.[7] Biko was brutally tortured and murdered, and many in the Black Consciousness movement were either exiled or imprisoned. Workers in what was to become the Congress of South African Trade Unions (COSATU) engaged in what were then illegal strikes. These strikes became increasingly political, demanding the end of the oppressive government. By the late 1980s, the United Democratic Front had been formed, and the slogan of the ANC, "make the country ungovernable", went from being rhetoric to a reality. Throughout this time, the ANC in exile, under the leadership of Oliver Tambo, had initiated a number of campaigns, including before the United Nations, to muster support for the struggle against apartheid. And then there was the war on the border of Angola.[8] It was a long and difficult armed struggle, as well as constant mass uprisings, that ultimately led to the National Party's conclusion that they had no choice but to negotiate with the ANC, and move to a government that would at least include the majority population in some capacity. But what capacity?

The negotiations for the Constitution were difficult. From 1992 to 1994, there was continual violence in the townships. It was unclear that the negotiations would be successful, and the fragility of the process was always underscored by the violent tensions between different groups in the liberation struggle.[9] Albie Sachs played a major role in these negotiations, known as the Convention for a Democratic South Africa (CODESA). In 1992, the negotiations broke down, and there was some question as to whether or not they would be able to continue. CODESA was replaced by the Multiparty Negotiating Forum in 1993, which ultimately ratified an interim constitution. But even these negotiations were fraught with violence. In 1993, a right-wing group attacked the building in which the negotiations were taking place, and actually held the building for a period of time. In that same year, one of the heroes of the liberation struggle, South African Communist Party leader

Chris Hani, was assassinated. Rather than a miracle, it was determination and courage that made the new South Africa possible and led to the adoption of what is one of the most progressive constitutions in the world, a constitution that explicitly commits itself to the transformation of the oppressive relations of apartheid.

The negotiated settlement was made possible only by a revolutionary struggle. What is often forgotten is that there was a revolution in South Africa, which Emeritus Justice Laurie Ackermann has called a "substantive revolution".[10] A substantive revolution is a phrase adopted by the German legal theorist Hans Kelsen. He distinguished between a procedural and a substantive revolution. Kelsen's procedural revolution is the kind of revolution we are used to, where the revolutionary party seizes state power, ends the existing government entirely, firing or punishing all those who participated in it, and begins an entirely new nation state. A substantive revolution, on the other hand, is one in which the government in power is not completely overthrown, but rather, there is a legal transformation of the existing state structure.[11] In order to have such a legal transformation, the party in power has to give up its right to rule, and that, in a profound sense, is what the National Party did when it entered into negotiations with the ANC. But there is another aspect of the substantive revolution that is relevant to South Africa, which is that all those who participated in the former government, whether as justices or civil servants, were not simply fired. Nor were all the laws simply wiped off the books. Instead, a complicated constitutional solution was sought that would ensure transformation of the legal and political structure of the country, but would do so within constitutional means. And yet the commitment to transformation is made explicit in the Constitution. To quote the preamble of the Constitution:

> We, the people of South Africa,
> Recognise the injustices of our past;
> Honour those who suffered for justice and freedom in our land;
> Respect those who have worked to build and develop our country; and
> Believe that South Africa belongs to all who live in it, united in our diversity.
> We therefore, through our freely elected representatives, adopt this Constitution as the supreme law of the Republic so as to
>
> - Heal the divisions of the past and establish a society based on democratic values, social justice and fundamental human rights;
> - Lay the foundations for a democratic and open society in which government is based on the will of the people and every citizen is equally protected by law;
> - Improve the quality of life of all citizens and free the potential of each person; and

- Build a united and democratic South Africa able to take its rightful place as a sovereign state in the family of nations.[12]

The South African Constitution includes socio-economic rights as fully enforceable.[13] This is a break with many constitutions, even those that recognize some form of socio-economic rights, in that these rights are given equal status to the more familiar, civil constitutional rights.[14] Many militants and revolutionaries had been suspicious of constitutions or even a bill of rights, precisely because they did not protect socio-economic rights, and therefore could become a bad excuse for the protection of massively unjust private property distribution in the name of the so-called protection of personhood.[15] The Constitution of South Africa protects the right to housing, the right to healthcare, food, water, and social security, and the right to education. The Constitution also protects environmental rights, and these rights, too, are given equal status with the more traditional civil rights we associate with a constitution.[16] Almost all of the programmatic suggestions that have been made in the Anglo-American and European academic universe when it comes to multiculturalism have been incorporated into the South African Constitution.[17] Affirmative action is protected in a complex equality clause that actually seeks to avoid the dilemma of so-called reverse discrimination that has been used time and time again in the United States to create a barrier to the much-needed transformation of the basic institutions that have enforced racial oppression throughout history.[18]

Such a far-reaching constitution demands a rich and complicated jurisprudence, because there are no templates for a constitution that goes beyond what is often thought of as fundamental to the rule of law. The South African Constitution is the only constitution in the world that explicitly mandates direct horizontal application of constitutional rights.[19] Direct horizontal application is the application of constitutional rights between private parties, so that the traditional notion of state action is, on the face of the Constitution, not necessary for someone to press a constitutional right against another citizen in the new South Africa. The reason for this was that the ANC was worried that without direct horizontal application of the Constitution, apartheid would be privatized. Again, since this is the only constitution in the world that has direct horizontal application, it has been controversial, and even ridiculed by some legal scholars.[20] Twenty years into the new dispensation, the Constitutional Court of South Africa has struggled to realize the high ideals of this constitution — high ideals that are inseparable from the transformation demanded by a substantive revolution.

Our book is entitled, *From Revolutionary Activist to Constitutional Court Judge*. It is rare to have the words "revolutionary" and "jurisprudence" put together in a sentence, let alone in the title of a book. But we have already seen that part of what makes South Africa unique is that it was a substantive revolution which dared a kind of complexity in the transformation of the country, a complexity that can be avoided in the more recognizable procedural revolution. Thus, law, in a profound sense, and legal transformation have been reconnected in the context of the new South Africa.

But can there be a revolutionary legality based on a system of members of the revolutionary struggle having rights, prior to the adoption of a new constitution? Albie Sachs not only argues that there can be, but in fact insists that there was an approach to having rights within the revolution that guided even the most difficult moments of the armed struggle. To quote him:

> For my part, I was convinced that if in the 1980s and earlier, we had not taken principled positions on questions of who "the enemy" was, what methods of struggle were legitimate and how torture was to be prohibited, we would not have achieved what many today regard as the most progressive Constitution in the world. We had in effect created a Bill of Rights at the heart of our struggle, asserting in practical ways our determination to retain our honor and dignity as freedom fighters, and to re-affirm the principles of justice on which the struggle was founded. It had accordingly not been difficult to move to a constitutional order in a free South Africa based on these very same principles. Our Constitution, then, had deep roots in concepts that had guided us in struggle. It was made by ourselves on our own soil, after patiently following the most inclusive process possible. And its well-honed text, a product of six years of intense negotiations outside and inside Parliament, and finalized after review by our Court according to agreed principles, gave us the instrument to deal with some of the most difficult problems of our era.[21]

We have much more to say about the details of the effort to develop just rules of conduct for the armed struggle in South Africa. That this may seem like a contradiction in terms is what makes it so important. Simply put: the ANC, in seeking to impose legal limits on itself, even at a time of bloody struggle, rejected the Stalinist idea that the ends justified the means. The means of the struggle had to be regulated in accordance with the ideals of the struggle. So in a very deep sense, Sachs was right to argue that his journey was one from an idealistic young freedom fighter to a lawyer working on jurisprudence for the revolution to a judge whose job was to realize in law the great ideals of the Constitution. It is important to face squarely the need for revolutionary jurisprudence in the context of an armed struggle or even militant mass movements. As in the case of the idea of a substantive revolution, South Africa demands that we deepen our understanding of what a revolution is, and confront directly the complexity of revolutionary struggle in the twenty-first century.

Often, the complexity of revolutionary struggle, or even uncertainty as to the meaning of revolution, has led some thinkers to simply reject the idea of revolution altogether. Rather than attempting to build a new nation state, we create local communities of resistance that find ways to disrupt the powers that be. But a substantive revolution is still a revolution. Apartheid had to be undone. Apartheid had to be overthrown. And this could only be done if a new nation state and a new government were put in the place of the old. It would have made a mockery of the suffering of the black majority to argue that they could, within apartheid, create communities of resistance. Such communities would have been immediately repressed, and their members sent to prison. So again, South Africa makes us think about what it means to hold on to the idea of revolution, hold on to the transformation of an entire nation state in the name of justice, and yet do so with the clarity of mind to face all the complexities of what revolutions might entail, and that they may no longer look like the procedural revolutions described by Hans Kelsen.[22]

Sachs has written that the famous Truth and Reconciliation Commission (TRC) in South Africa actually grew out of the jurisprudence for the revolution that was developed during the armed struggle.[23] People in the struggle were called to take responsibility for their actions, and Sachs, as we will see in the course of this book, played a major role in drawing up the rules of conduct that legalized the meaning of that responsibility. Again, the South African TRC went beyond other such commissions in allowing as many people as was feasible to come forward and tell their story. Can a Truth and Reconciliation Commission of this sort developed in South Africa be considered part of an effort to develop a revolutionary jurisprudence? We think the question is an extremely important one, and again, it is one of the reasons for which we felt the urgency of putting together this book.

Nelson Mandela was released from prison in 1990. This was a year after the fall of the Berlin Wall, which became a huge symbol of the supposed end of the communist dream. Questions were raised as to what should happen to high-ranking members of the communist parties in many of the so-called former communist states. Certainly, the party was not to remain as part of the government. But that is not what happened in South Africa. The South African Communist Party, COSATU, and the ANC are the three purportedly equal parties of the government. The Communist Party played a proud role in the historic armed struggle and in the militant uprisings in the late 1970s and 1980s. Indeed, when Mandela came out of jail, he committed himself to all the socialist goals that were present in the Freedom Charter of 1956. Commentators have argued that Mandela stepped away from those goals, as did the ANC.[24] A full discussion of whether or not the ANC capitulated completely to the demands of neoliberal capitalism is beyond the scope of this introduction, as is the huge question of whether the South African Constitution is even compatible with capitalism.[25] For our purposes here, we simply want to emphasize that the literature that focuses exclusively on the transition from so-called communism to capitalism simply is not rich or complex enough to cover the example of South Africa, and that is one more reason why South Africa is important to the thinking of revolution and radical transformation. Members of the Communist Party remain part of the government, and the Communist Party, though challenged from the Right and the Left, is recognized as one of the three reigning parties of the coalition. No one can come to terms with the complex history of the revolutionary struggle in South Africa if we try to fit it into the neat box of what happens when a society or nation state is in transition from an authoritarian capitalist state to a constitutional democracy with profound social commitments. Therefore, the Fukuyamas of the world who have declared the end of the big ideals run up against the example of South Africa in all of its complexity and messiness.[26] The majority of South Africans continue to fight for an ideal, to realize the promise of a truly transformed society, one that is transformed in the name of justice.

The legal and jurisprudential journey of Albie Sachs, which we discuss in this book, takes one into the throes of the struggle to live up to the great ideals of the South African Constitution. As he himself reflects:

> It is not only the dignity of the poor that is assailed when homeless people are driven from pillar to post in a desperate quest for a place where they and their families can rest their heads. Our society as a whole is demeaned when state action intensifies rather than mitigates their marginalization.[27]

We humbly offer this book as an attempt to grapple with the jurisprudence that fearlessly takes on the mandate to do justice in a country that remains fraught with all forms of injustice, including severe economic inequality.

Chapter 1

Comrade judge: can a revolutionary be a judge?

Drucilla Cornell

It is an honor to have this opportunity to engage critically with the political and moral philosophy of Emeritus Justice Albie Sachs, and with his significant contributions to the development of the constitutional jurisprudence of the new South Africa. I will first discuss Sachs's history as a participant in the struggle to overthrow apartheid and the attempt to replace it with a just society. Sachs was an African National Congress (ANC) member, and as a lawyer and law professor, he was involved with articulating, defending, and helping to institutionalize ethical and quasi-legal limits on the armed struggle itself. In other words, Sachs engaged in a careful analysis and critique of the role of law and of ethical limitation in revolutionary struggles long before he became a judge. Sachs played a major role in arguing and developing a Code of Conduct that went against the grain of revolutionary movements that practised the idea that if a war was just, the means to promote the just ends were automatically legitimate, including the most brutal means, such as torture. From the beginning, then, Sachs has been thinking about the role of ethics and law in revolution in a way that is almost unique, because he was doing so in the course of an armed struggle. Sachs himself had been a fighter in the underground, but not as an armed combatant. Yet he was clearly part of an organization that felt it had no other choice than to commit itself to armed violence. I will examine the relation between Sachs's early work as a revolutionary and his constitutional jurisprudence by introducing Étienne Balibar's notion of "civility," a principle of anti-violence which I will connect with Sachs's recent defense of the role of uBuntu-botho in the contemporary jurisprudence of South Africa.[1]

Following a number of other thinkers, including Emeritus Justice Laurie Ackermann, I will argue that South Africa had a "substantive revolution," and that Sachs has made a major contribution to a jurisprudence worthy of both words in that phrase: "substantive" and "revolution."[2] The phrase "substantive revolution" comes from Hans Kelsen, who argued that there were two kinds of revolution.[3] What Kelsen labeled a "full procedural revolution" is the kind of revolution we are most familiar with: the revolutionary party seizes state power and completely overthrows the government. Practically, this means that all the laws, all the officials, and all institutions of the government are liquidated as part of the old order — sometimes, unfortunately, literally liquidated, in that the officials are executed — and that an entirely new order is established with new laws, new officials, and new institutions. By contrast, a substantive revolution is one in which the ruling party legally transfers power to the revolutionary party or parties. The moment when the South African National Party voted itself out of power by entering into negotiations and finally getting the racist Parliament to legislate the new non-racial, democratic constitutional order, may be the only example in the world of what Kelsen might have considered a truly substantive revolution.[4] One reason why the new South Africa has captured the imagination of so many activists and revolutionaries around the world seems to be that it is this other *kind* of revolution, and whether or not it falters may indicate whether or not this kind of substantive revolution is workable. Often, the Court has used the metaphor of the bridge as a way to understand the transition from the past to the future. Whether or not one likes this metaphor — it was often used as a justification for the Truth and Reconciliation Commission (TRC), which, amongst other things, controversially gave amnesty to perpetrators of the worst kinds of crimes if they came forward with the truth — it at least points to a notion of revolution that does not seek to simply obliterate the past, but instead to morally disenfranchise it, which in the case of South Africa means something extremely complicated.

The famous "peaceful transition" is somewhat of a misnomer, since it came after an extended armed struggle, as well as wars on the borders of Angola and Namibia. Yet the ultimate transition took place through negotiations, including negotiations over the foundational principles for the new Constitution. The question raised by Kelsen, which the new Constitution and constitutional dispensation had to envision, is: what is the substance of the revolution, if it does not literally "do in" the old government and start a brand new one? If it is truly revolutionary in the moral and ethical sense, it promises a new moral order based on all the ideals and values that were completely negated, not only by apartheid, but by the economic system of super-exploitation and subordination that went with it. This kind of revolution is extremely complicated, and one key to understanding the first 15 years of constitutional jurisprudence in the new South Africa is the attempt to give meaning to what the substantive revolution would be in a dispensation committed, as Sachs often tells us, to dignity, freedom, and equality for all.

It is important to note, as I wrote earlier, that a substantive revolution in its second demand, which is for a revolutionary break with the old ethical order and the creation of a new ethical order, is not one for which there are rules or a blueprint by which what has happened in South Africa can be neatly judged. If one looks at the economic realities of South Africa, it would be only too easy to say that the revolution has failed, and that South Africa is just one more example of how neoliberal capitalism destroys any aspirations to an alternative ideal of economic development in the name of justice. Clearly, the reigning faction in the ANC has moved away from socialism, even as it is equally clear that on-the-ground movements have not done so. The relationship between the Constitutional Court's attempts to configure a new ethical order and these mass movements is complex indeed.[5] My claim is a more modest one: that the Constitutional Court has taken seriously its legal and moral mandate that a substantive change in the ethical reality of South Africa — what Hegel would have called *Sittlichkeit* — must be a guiding aspiration to all of the Court's work. This is a different claim from the question of whether the Court has "failed" or "succeeded" in realizing a substantive revolution, precisely because the project of configuring what such an ethical transformation would mean is obviously ongoing, and one that, of course, runs into the severe limitations placed upon it by the brutal realities of neoliberal capitalism. The big question beyond the scope of this chapter is: to what degree the aspiration to *Gleichheit in Recht* (equality in right) disrupts the material demands of neoliberal capitalism. Even though I cannot dare to answer this question here — this would take us through a reworking of Marx's critique of Hegel — I think that we can at least see in Sachs's jurisprudence, and in the work of most if not all of the judges on this Court, a commitment to ethical transformation in the name of a critical telos regulated by the ideal of dignity and its corresponding ideals of freedom and equality.

I will also raise some questions as to whether or not the Constitutional Court and Sachs, with their important regard for the limits of the judiciary, have pushed the ethical and political principles of the Constitution far enough to challenge the establishment of a system of neoliberal capitalism as the main model of economic development, which may dangerously undermine the commitment of the Constitution to what Étienne Balibar has called "equaliberty," the radical identification of freedom and equality.[6] In the Freedom Charter of the ANC, the notion of a just society was inseparable from the struggle for an alternative to capitalism, whether one was to think about that as either social democracy or democratic socialism. Famously, the Bill of Rights in South Africa protects socio-economic rights as on a par with the more standard liberal rights. However, these rights include the phrase "within its available resources" in the enumeration of the rights themselves. For example, the right to housing reads as follows: "26(1) Everyone has the right to have adequate housing; (2) The state must take reasonable legislative and other measures, within its available resources, to achieve the progressive realization of this right."[7] But the question arises as to how resources could be made more available by alternative systems of economic development. It is of course not the role of any constitutional court to develop detailed plans of economic development. But the question still remains whether the South African Constitutional Court, under its ideals of civility and equaliberty, which I will defend as uBuntu-botho, should go further than it has to challenge specific policies and economic legislation that would make the limitation of resources inevitable. In this chapter I will draw heavily from Sachs's recent judicial autobiography, *The Strange Alchemy of Life and Law*.[8] The reason I rely on this autobiography to the extent that I do is that is draws the connection between the ANC's attempt to "civilize" the armed struggle — as implausible as such an effort might seem — and Sachs's own role in developing a jurisprudence, including a jurisprudence of uBuntu-botho, which at least aspires to regulate itself in accordance with one of Étienne Balibar's critical concepts of politics: civility. In other words, it is not simply Justice Sachs himself — although he played a major role in the development of the Code of Conduct in the armed struggle — that is central here, but, more importantly, the attempt at least to recognize that violence can never be a neutral means, and that the politics of the armed struggle itself will ultimately, for better or worse, infect the society that is to be created after a revolutionary shift in power.

The ethical limitation of violence: civilizing the revolution, civilizing the state

Emeritus Justice Albie Sachs became a freedom fighter at a very young age, and suffered for it. As a young practising lawyer, he was detained in solitary confinement for three months under what was called the "ninety day law," which allowed suspects to be locked up in solitary confinement without any charge being brought against them. Sachs describes how horrifying it was to survive in solitary confinement:

> How difficult it was to be brave! Before it happens, you think that when you are locked up you simply bare your chest, retain belief in your cause, and hold out forever. The reality is totally different. You are living in a little concrete cube. You stare at your toes, you stare at the wall. Your toes, the wall, your toes, the wall, you do not know how long it is going to last. There is nothing to do. There is no one to speak to. It is an inhuman existence.[9]

Sachs described how he kept himself "human" by scratching marks on the wall, making up songs to sing to himself, and doing anything he could to give himself a sense that this would soon be over, and that he had remained human throughout. On the ninetieth day he was released, and had barely had a minute to celebrate his freedom when he was arrested and detained again, this time for 78 days. Two years later, he was detained once more. This time he was subjected to torture by sleep deprivation. One of the crucial points in Sachs's argument against torture is that it is always about dehumanizing the tortured person, and it cannot be anything else. Simply put, therefore, it is always wrong. Sachs describes how the information his torturers sought to obtain was already out of date. He gives us his own description of torture as follows:

> It was the worst, worst moment of my life. It was not a hypothetical situation of the kind that some academics conjure up when discussing the costs and benefits of the government using torture. And, as in 99.9 per cent of cases where forms of torture are used, there was no ticking bomb nearby when I collapsed on the floor, they poured water on me, and they lifted me up. I still remember those thick, heavy fingers prying my eyes open. I collapsed again, more water, the shoes shuffling around me, some brown, some black and their sense of quiet, methodical urgency, the muted triumph as they were now breaking through my resistance. Any information I had at that stage was stale. Possibly they wanted to get me to be a witness against somebody who had also been in the resistance. That would have been a double triumph, because I could then have been projected as a traitor, as an instrument of the very state I had been opposing. They wanted hegemony, dominance, power, control, mastery. The practice was systematic, it was organized, it was condoned, it was part of policy.[10]

Sachs learned he would be considered by his own government to be a terrorist: he went into exile as one, and was explicitly labeled as such. He found out that he was a "terrorist" when he was denied a visa to attend a conference in the United States. Only because Washington changed its policy on the struggle in South Africa was the designation of terrorist dropped, at least for the purposes of visiting the United States. We often hear the phrase that someone's freedom fighter is someone else's terrorist, and the word "terrorist" is notoriously hard to define. Sometimes, the definition turns on the question of whether or not one believes that the struggle in which the so-called terrorist is involved is one, as in the case of the ANC, for justice and against a crime for humanity, apartheid. However, Sachs's own experience of terrorism not only led him to condemn it as absolutely wrong — no further discussion needed — but also led to his understanding that revolutionary movements that are fighting for rights and justice must be limited by the very ethical ideals they stand for, even if they have no choice but to engage in an armed struggle. Sachs set an ethical limitation on the armed struggle, which would separate that struggle from terrorism:

> What made it particularly ironical that we should be punished as terrorists, and in some ways made it especially dreadful, was the fact we were actually strongly against terrorism. In the late 1960s and early 1970s, there were "isms" all over the place. Capitalism, socialism, imperialism, Stalinism, Trotskyism — only social democracy didn't fit into the "isms." And one of the "isms" that we had denounced on principle in our

> movement was terrorism. To respond in kind to the violence of apartheid was just wrong. Terrorism was based on the use of indiscriminate violence, directed at civilian people because they happened to belong to a particular group, race, or community. It was totally lacking in political intelligence. It was completely antithetical to our ideals. We were fighting for justice against the system of white supremacy, not against a race.[11]

What makes Sachs's own history as a revolutionary so important is not only that he had a personal moral code against torture, but that he was asked to write a Code of Conduct for the armed struggle in South Africa, which may be the only armed struggle in the world that developed a detailed Code of Conduct for itself. Sachs argued that the person who tortures loses his humanity:

> What does terrorism do to those who use it? What kind of person do you become? How could you claim to be a freedom fighter when you kill indiscriminately? I am sure that was the underlying morality, sometimes stated, sometimes implicit. And it was a morality of justice that turned out to be strong, not weak. It constituted a powerful unifying force inside the ANC, enabling it to survive thirty years of exile with no major disputes or breakups, at a time when virtually all other exile movements splintered.[12]

When Sachs was Director of Research at the Ministry of Justice of Mozambique, Oliver Tambo asked him to come to Lusaka, Zambia, where the ANC had its headquarters. Tambo told him that in cases when the ANC believed they were dealing with security forces who had infiltrated their organization, they were occasionally using torture to get information from them. Tambo asked Sachs to write up a Code of Conduct that would absolutely forbid torture. This Code of Conduct, given the democratic principles of the ANC, was then passed out to as many people as possible, both in exile and in the underground, and the various opinions of the different branches were discussed at a conference in Kabwe, Zambia. Sachs's Code of Conduct is extremely elaborate, and he describes it as follows:

> I remember the debate vividly. There was overwhelming support for the Code of Conduct as a whole. The delegates were happy with the idea of classifying offences against the organization into three categories, each with its own form of investigation, its own procedures and its own penalties. This presupposed graduated responses to three main categories of people: those who were merely unduly disruptive at branch meetings; those who drove while drunk, or committed offences such as assaults or theft or abuse of women; and those who allegedly had been sent into the organization in order to kill its leaders and wreck its functioning.

> Tribunals akin to courts were established for the second and third categories, with judicial officers who would be independent, as well as the equivalent of prosecutors and defense counsel, and a right of appeal. It was clear at the conference that the idea of establishing an appropriate system of legality inside the organization strongly appealed to the members.[13]

One of the most difficult questions was whether or not there could be circumstances that were so exceptional that torture could be justified, and the answer was an emphatic no. Sachs emphasizes that the participants in this conference sometimes risked their lives to attend the meeting at all. The frightful circumstances of the conference underscored the precariousness of the continuing existence of the ANC. Still, as Sachs emphasizes, it was the soldiers in the struggle whose lives were constantly on the line, who insisted:

> They didn't enter the realms of reasoning of some who speak about where and when to draw the line. Can you torture someone to death because of a ticking bomb? Can you use electrodes or water suffocation, or sleep deprivation? The young soldiers — and the not-so-young-lawyers — were making unambiguous statements about the kind of people we were, what we were fighting for, and what our morality and core values were about. They had seen in practice how torture had dehumanized not only the tortured, but the torturers themselves, transforming people who had been their friends, who had left school and university with them to join the freedom struggle, into behaving like brutes. In dealing with brutes, they had allowed themselves to become brutalized, even if only for brief spells. The speakers were adamant. They did not want to belong to an organization that used torture. Full stop.[14]

The Code of Conduct was passed, and as Sachs emphasizes, every attempt was made to live by it. But of course, in any armed struggle, there are moments of failure due to fear and a sense of emergency, and those failures were noted by the ANC, particularly as they involved certain wrongs committed against enemy combatants on the borders of Angola in what was indeed a war. According to Sachs, one of the inspirations for the TRC was that the ANC felt it necessary to come to terms with its own failures to live up to the Code of Conduct and the principles of the Freedom Charter. Sachs went through an assassination attempt himself, and was ultimately able to shake hands with someone closely involved with this attempt.

This event alone demonstrates how committed he is to what Étienne Balibar calls "civility." Balibar has introduced the notion of civility as an important addition to two other crucial concepts of politics: emancipation and transformation. He defines civility in a preliminary way as a principle of antiviolence:

Albie Sachs reading the Code of Conduct

Source: Albie Sachs documentary collection at the Mayibuye Centre.

> Civility . . . is certainly not a politics which suppresses all violence; but it excludes extremes of violence, so as to *create a* (public, private) *space* for politics (emancipation, transformation), and enable violence itself to be historicized.[15]

Balibar argues: "It is not only the state or the economy that needs to be 'civilized' or to become 'civil,' but also revolution itself."[16] I want to emphasize that long before the ANC was voted into power as the majority party, it sought to integrate something like civility from the bottom up, if we take seriously that there truly was a democratic process in the passage of the Code of Conduct during the struggle. Clearly, what was needed here was not a principle of non-violence, since no one in that meeting denied the need for armed struggle and for having an underground army: Umkhonto We Sizwe (Spear of the Nation). So at least on its face, the Code of Conduct comes very close to incorporating a notion of civility that did work from the bottom up.

Of course, given that Sachs became a Justice in the Constitutional Court, he was later explicitly engaged in the institutionalization of civility into the law of the new dispensation. Thus, he accepts something close to what Balibar discusses as the role of civility in Hegel's own understanding of the *Rechtsstaat*:

> Hegel's idea of civility is the counterpart to his dialectical conviction that, in history, violence is convertible ("the real is rational"), provided it is preventively processed [*traitée*] by a state which is, itself, a *Rechtsstaat* — that is to say, a state which constitutes itself with the intention of liberating individuals. And the kernel of this is the exposition of a process of reciprocal mediation between the particular and the universal enabling the individual to *belong* to multiple (family, regional, religious, occupational, political . . .) "communities", and hence to maintain *concrete* identities — and the "honor" of those identities — while acquiring (by law, education, public functions and social citizenship) a universal — or, better, universalizing — abstract identity which superimposes itself upon the preceding ones, and becomes their condition of possibility. More precisely, Hegel's idea is that primary identities and senses of belonging have to be virtually destroyed in order to be not purely and simply eliminated, but reconstructed as particular expressions and mediations of collective political identity, or a belonging to the state.[17]

Balibar argues — and I agree with him — that the Hegelian idea of a universalizing citizenship at the very least implies a moment of disidentification and reidentification which changes the nature of previously established identities. In South Africa, this process of disidentification and reidentification is not as ruthless as it is in Hegel, if one reads Hegel as radically reconstructing all prior forms of belonging and identification in the name of a complex mediated relationship to the state rooted in freedom. Yet there is little doubt that the "material" of the Constitution requires something like this process of disidentification and reidentification, because certain forms of identification are rendered legally suspect by the ideals of the Constitution themselves. Sachs names the overarching ideal of the *Rechtsstaat* of South Africa "dignitarianism," which he contrasts with both libertarianism and communitarianism, as it has come to be understood in much of the theoretical writing of Anglo-American political philosophy.[18] But what is important to note is that for Sachs, dignitarianism, as a regulative ideal of the whole Constitution, turns on the development of a new narrative of what the state stands for and how people belong to it, which, as I am suggesting, has a Hegelian ring to it. Sachs writes:

> On an individual basis and between all communities we have a long way to go, but at the national level we now, for the first time, have a single narrative, a common history of the most painful moments of the recent past. You cannot have a country with different memories and expect a sense of common citizenship to grow. You cannot have a white history and a black history that have nothing to do with each other, except that they overlap in time and place. You have to have a single, broad, commonly accepted narrative of the country's history.[19]

Of course, many critics would disagree with Sachs that the TRC effectively created a shared narrative, and would argue instead that there was a master drama at play that actually silenced many who came before the TRC to testify to their own suffering.[20] I agree with the central critique made by many who noted the profound flaws of the TRC. At the same time, however, I think that we could make a more modest claim that the TRC, with all its failings, represented an acknowledgement of a past that had to be addressed and, therefore, despite the containment of the anguish and profound trauma of those who testified, there was still a recognition of a necessary break with what had gone before. When there is any form of acknowledgement of something as horrendous as apartheid, and the official story that justified it begins to collapse, there is also inevitably resistance to that acknowledgement. But somewhat paradoxically, this resistance is itself a kind of acknowledgement. Of course, whether there was actually a revolutionary break remains a huge question, and I will return to it when I discuss the substantive revolution as a critical framework for analyzing the quest for a new South Africa. I emphasize the word quest because, as we will see shortly, a substantive revolution is not one that can be held accountable against a blueprint of rules, but instead evokes a set of ideals as aspirations to a new ethical order that are constantly being reconfigured.

At the level of law, Sachs has engaged seriously with feminist critiques about how the notion of a reasonable person carried within it masculine biases. In a creative manner, Sachs develops the notion of a "reasonable South African," which of course is part and parcel of the narration of what the word "new" means in the constitutional dispensation. He does so in deciding whether a ban on the sale of liquor on Sundays and Christian Good Friday violated the freedom of religion protected by the Constitution. Sachs wrote a separate judgment from the majority, in order to draw out the meaning of a different concept of reasonableness, which is in a profound sense connected with the grounding ideal of dignitarianism of the whole Constitutional dispensation:

> In testing whether in the present case the State endorsed a particular set of beliefs in a manner which violated the right of religious freedom, I shall attempt to apply the sensibilities and perspectives neither of what has been called the "reasonable Christian" nor, for example, of the reasonable Jew, Muslim, or Hindu, nor of the reasonable atheist, but of the reasonable South African (of any faith or of none) who is neither hypersensitive nor overly insensitive to the belief in question, but highly attuned to the requirements of the Constitution. In my opinion, such a reasonable South African is a person of common sense immersed in the cultural realities of our country and aware of the amplitude and nuanced nature of our Constitution. He or she neither attempts relentlessly to purge public life of even the faintest association with religion for fear of

> otherwise descending the slippery slope to theocracy, nor at the other extreme, regards the religiously-based practices of the past to be as natural and non-sectarian as the air one breathes simply because of their widespread acceptance.[21]

It is important to note here, of course, that for Sachs, the appeal to an open and democratic society rooted in dignitarianism is an ideal, not one that has been realized in history, as Hegel argued in his philosophical defense of the *Rechtsstaat*. In Sachs's own quote, he seems to be appealing to a kind of pragmatic Hegelianism, in that this ideal is historically rooted in societies that have been hailed as democratic. Of course, given the brute realities of many of those countries in terms of their own failure to realize anything like a truly democratic society, or even adhere to the most rudimentary respect for the dignity of all of its citizens, this form of pragmatic Hegelianism would seem to be severely lacking in rigor. I would agree that we are not looking to any historically realized ideal, particularly in a neoliberal capitalist society like the United States, or even the so-called social democracies of Europe. That said, we can and should interpret Sachs somewhat differently, as defending a regulative ideal that has not been realized anywhere, but which should pull us towards trying to develop the coherence of values and ideals demanded by the *Rechtsstaat*. But this understanding, of course, means that the development of "coherence" is always a constructive project that outlines an orientation and a set of ethical considerations, rather than, as in Hegel, an attempt to sketch the foundations of a philosophy of right, at least on the level of actuality, as having a coherent structure that has unfolded in a philosophically justified history. Given the reality of the continuing fractures in the new South Africa, the appeal to the reasonable South African may at first blush seem to be naive idealism. However, we can see such an appeal differently if we understand that some conception of the reasonable is inherent in the idea of a *Rechtsstaat*, and should be interpreted within the moral and legal mandate of the new Constitution. Thus, for Sachs, the reasonable new South African is integral to aspirational ideals of the constitutional dispensation, and articulates a moral as well as a legal mandate inseparable from the critical framework provided by the idea of a substantive revolution.

That dignitarianism is an ideal has major implications for the way in which Sachs thinks about the role of judging as a judge. As he explains:

> Such a society is a notional one. It is not to be found in this country or that. It does not have this particular constitution or that, this kind of judiciary or that. It is an ideal type of society, constructed out of the actual experience of the way issues of power and of rights are dealt with in countries that are widely regarded as democratic. This society repudiates forms of oppression, hardship, division and discrimination that have been known in the past (and, sadly, are still current in many parts of the world

> today). It acknowledges the foundational character of the principle of human dignity, and aspires to accept people for who they are. It presupposes diversity and welcomes and treats everyone with equal concern and respect. It is a society that protects rights of conscience and speech. It is one that ensures that government is accountable to the people, that every vote counts equally, and that minority voices can be heard.[22]

Famously, the first judgment rendered by the Constitutional Court, the *Makwanyane* case, outlawed the death penalty in the name of a substantive moral change in the ethical foundations of the new society, which needed to be recognized in constitutional law.[23] In the *Azapo* case, the Court upheld conditional amnesty for those persons who came forward with the truth of their actions before the TRC. This granting of conditional amnesty had been challenged by the Azanian People's Organisation, together with families of other victims, who argued that this amnesty took away their right to seek criminal or civil redress in the court system. The Court quoted the epilogue of the Constitution in order to undergird the importance for the new South Africa of the TRC and its aspiration for non-vengeful ways of truth seeking, despite the many retrospective critiques of what it actually achieved. Both the *Makwanyane* and the *Azapo* decisions are well known, and Justice Sachs rightly argues that they are foundational for the new dispensation. But Sachs emphasizes that two lesser known cases indicate how deeply a conversionist anti-violence principle lies at the basis of the substantive revolution in South Africa. These cases indicate that what makes the use of such a principle so sweeping in the new South Africa is that it not only founds a new dispensation for the nation state, but also implies the responsibility of the Constitutional Court to uphold an anti-violence principle on a transnational or international plane.[24]

In the *Mohamed* case, a man entered South Africa under an assumed name and applied for asylum. He was charged with an act of terrorism, which involved the bombing of the US embassy of Tanzania. The South African Government worked with the FBI of the United States to apprehend him on the basis of an arrest warrant that had been issued for him in connection with the bombing. The South African authorities handed him over to the US Government. On his arrival in the United States, he was charged with a number of criminal offenses in relation to the bombing, and if he was found guilty, he could be put to death. The Court argued that the South African Government erred, particularly the immigration officials involved in the case, for handing Mohamed over to the US Government without an assurance that he would not be subjected to the death penalty. In this sense, then, the South African Constitutional Court, even if it had been preceded by a similar decision in Germany, insisted on a principle of anti-cruelty not only within the boundaries of South Africa, but within a country that is known for its ruthless implementation of the death penalty. Here we have someone accused of terrorism in which a number of people lost their lives, and Mohamed was not even a citizen of South Africa. However, the Constitution's anti-violence principle here protects the human being beyond the boundaries of a nation state in which that particular person had come to seek asylum:

> The Court declared: That is a serious finding. South Africa is a young democracy still finding its way to full compliance with the values and ideals enshrined in the Constitution. It is therefore important that the State lead by example. This principle cannot be put better than in the celebrated words of Justice Brandeis in *Olmstead et al v United States*: "In a government of laws, existence of the government will be imperilled if it fails to observe the law scrupulously . . . Government is the potent, omnipresent teacher. For good or for ill, it teaches the whole people by its example . . . If the Government becomes a law-breaker, it breeds contempt for the law; it invites every man to become a law unto himself; it invites anarchy." The warning was given in a distant era but remains as cogent as ever. Indeed, for us in this country, it has a particular relevance: we saw in the past what happens when the State bends the law to its own ends and now, in the new era of constitutionality, we may be tempted to use questionable measures in the war against crime.[25]

The *Kaunda* case involved the complicated issue of what responsibility the South African Government had to citizens of South Africa who were mercenaries captured in Zimbabwe, and who were faced with possibilities of torture and execution in Equatorial Guinea. Throughout his life, as we have seen, Sachs has emphasized that even a good end does not justify immoral means, and most especially not the use of mercenary soldiers. Yet despite Sachs's deep convictions on this point, he also was adamant that there was a duty on the part of the South African Government to do whatever it could to protect South African citizens when they are faced with a grossly unfair trial, execution, and torture, even when they are acting outside of South Africa, and certainly beyond the parameters of its law. To quote Sachs:

> The values of our Constitution and the human rights principles enshrined in international law are mutually reinforcing, interrelated and, where they overlap, indivisible. South Africa owes much of its very existence to the rejection of apartheid by the organized international community and the latter's concern for the upholding of fundamental human rights. It would be a strange interpretation of our Constitution that suggested that adherence by the government in any of its activities to the foundational norms that paved the way to its creation was merely an option and not a duty.
>
> In my opinion, the government has a clear and unambiguous duty to do whatever is reasonably within its power to prevent South Africans

> abroad, however grave their alleged offences, from being subjected to torture, grossly unfair trials and capital punishment. At the same time, the government must have an extremely wide discretion as to how best to provide what diplomatic protection it can offer.[26]

Sachs, rightly to my mind, puts the *Mahomed* case and the *Kaunda* case together, although they seem at first glance dissimilar, since the former involves a non-South African citizen and the latter is about South African citizens operating in a foreign country. What makes the *Kaunda* case particularly important is that many of those who tortured, killed, and maimed under apartheid now engage in those same activities as paid mercenaries in other countries. Sachs himself went through an assassination attempt, as we know, which left him without an arm and blind in one eye. And yet for Sachs, it is precisely here that a commitment to a new ethical relationship between people, enforced by law, is sorely tested, because of the temptation to turn against those who, on the face of things, deserve whatever they get.

Civility and uBuntu-botho

From the beginning of his work as a judge, Sachs has emphasized the central importance of giving center place to African interpretations of the values of the ideals of the Constitution, as well as giving pride and place to African ideals and values in their own right. In his concurring opinion to the *Makwyane* case, Sachs wrote:

> [365] Above all, however, it means giving long overdue recognition to African law and legal thinking as a source of legal ideas, values and practice. We cannot, unfortunately, extend the equality principle backwards in time to remove the humiliations and indignities suffered by past generations, but we can restore dignity to ideas and values that have long been suppressed or marginalized.

In that judgment, Sachs wrote, however, that it was not necessary to postpone the judgment because adequate documentation of African ideals had not been presented to the Court. He did so precisely because many of his colleagues developed their entire judgment through an analysis of what uBuntu-botho demanded of the new constitutional state. To quote Sachs:

> [374] . . . There does not appear to be any foundation for her plea that we postpone the matter. On the contrary, the materials that I will refer to point to a source of values entirely consistent with the overall thrust of the President's judgment, and, in particular, with his reference to the constitutionally acknowledged principle of *ubuntu*.

Justice Sachs has recently been evoking uBuntu-botho as a constitutive spirit of the substantive revolution, and as foundational for the new constitutional dispensation.[27] From 2005 until his retirement as a Justice, Sachs went on to become one of the most powerful advocates of uBuntu-Botho as a constitutional principle on the Constitutional Court of South Africa, even if he was initially unconvinced that uBuntu-botho could be a justifiable constitutional principle.[28] Nevertheless, I want to argue that the principle of anti-violence that I have traced in the ANC's Code of Conduct for the armed struggle and in the important judgments of the Constitutional Court discussed above — a principle which I have connected to what Hans Kelsen calls the "substantive revolution" and which I have interpreted in terms of Étienne Balibar's notion of civility — should in fact be *primarily* understood in terms of uBuntu-botho.

uBuntu-botho is an African principle of trans-individualism that can be considered the "law of law" or social bond. In uBuntu-botho, human beings are entwined in a work of ethical relations and obligations from the time they are born. Thus, the social bond is not a matter of separate individuals who, under different notions of either motivation or morality, come together at the cost of their absolute freedom in a state of nature. The inscription by the other, in the form of obligations, is not simply reduced to a social fact in which conventions and ethical behavior are rooted. Thus, it is a profound misunderstanding of uBuntu to confuse it with communitarianism, if communitarianism is understood as entailing an ontology of the community, and one which both encompasses the individual and limits the individual's rights. Under uBuntu-botho, it is only through the engagement and support of others that we can realize our own individuality, and come to be a fully developed person, whose uniqueness or singularity is inseparable from the long journey to moral and ethical development.

We can understand, then, that our ethical relationship to others is inseparable from how we are both embedded and supported by a community that is not outside us, but which is inscribed in us. The inscription of the other is also a principle of transcendence in the following sense: uBuntu-botho calls the individual out of him- or herself, back towards the ancestors, forwards towards the community, and further, towards ethical relations of mutual support of the potential of each one of us. Critics of uBuntu-botho have often mistaken it as an ethical ontology of a purportedly shared world. What is missed is the activism inherent in the notion of an ethical relation to the other, which is inseparable from the long struggle to become a unique being, in and through the support of others. Thus, uBuntu-botho clearly has an aspirational edge. There is no end to the struggle to bring about a humane world and to become a person in a humane world, who marks him or herself a singular being, precisely as the difference he or she makes in that effort.

Mabogo More brings together the different aspects of uBuntu in his own profound and yet succinct definition:

> In one sense uBuntu is a philosophical concept forming the basis of relationships, especially ethical behavior. In one sense, it is a traditional politico-ideological concept referring to socio-political action. As a moral or ethical concept, it is a point of view according to which moral practices are founded exclusively on consideration and enhancement of human well-being; a preoccupation with "human". It enjoins that what is morally good is what brings dignity, respect, contentment, and prosperity to others, self and the community at large. uBuntu is a demand for respect for persons no matter what their circumstances may be . . .
>
> In its politico-ideological sense it is a principle for all forms of social or political relationships. It enjoins and makes for peace and social harmony by encouraging the practice of sharing in all forms of communal existence.[29]

As both an ethical and a politico-ideological concept, uBuntu is always integral to the social bond. uBuntu-botho, then, encapsulates the moral and ethical relations demanded by human beings who must live together. But here is the key to understanding the complexity of uBuntu: uBuntu always moralizes social relations, and this moralization of social relations is what does not change about it. Human beings cannot be human without being inscribed in a moral and ethical world. But the actual ethical meaning of the world must change because of the aspirational aspect of uBuntu, in which we must strive to achieve a public good for all of us, and a shared world which not only abstractly respects the dignity of all others, but supports others in their unique capacity. Thus, as an ethical notion of the social bond that moralizes relationships, it is also always changing. A key example is that in the new South Africa, uBuntu-botho has been used to argue against gender inequality, while it may well have been used to support gender inequality in other circumstances hundreds of years ago.[30]

I submit that within the context of South Africa, uBuntu-botho should be underscored as the principle of anti-violence that converts extreme cruelty into an affirmative, ethical understanding of the social bond, not understood abstractly as a set of moral commands, but as a profound engagement with how our interrelatedness demands that we aspire to live together in accordance with a new meaning of how our humanness is shaped in that interaction. Sachs himself always emphasizes the interrelatedness of human beings as the basis for an ethical relationship, and so does uBuntu. It is not simply the ideal of humanity to which we aspire in Sachs, but a new ethical way of being together, which is then constitutionally defended as the basis of what brought South Africans together in the negotiation process, and what continues to tie them together in the struggle to bring a new ethical way of relating to one another into being. Since uBuntu-botho is a reflection on what it means to be human, it cannot stop at the borders of any particular country. Thus, the new state of South Africa not only had to stand behind its ideals within the boundaries of the new dispensation, but also to legally insist upon those ideals for other institutions within South Africa, such as the immigration authorities, and even for other nation states, who, within the terms of their own law, could justify the death penalty and even torture.

In one case, the *Masethla* case, Sachs explicitly connected civility with uBuntu-botho, insisting that these principles are in fact constitutional requirements. The case concerned the abrupt firing by the President of the country of the head of the national intelligence agency, in such a way that the latter's reputation was inevitably damaged. But it was not so much the reputation of the individual to which Sachs returns in his concurring judgment. Instead, he sought to emphasize that in a newly created constitution with new institutions, it is important for those in power to act in accordance not only with fairness, but with civility:

> Fair dealing and civility cannot be separated. Civility in a constitutional sense involves more than just courtesy or good manners. It is one of the binding elements of a constitutional democracy. It presupposes tolerance for those with whom one disagrees and respect for the dignity of those with whom one is in dispute. Civility, closely linked to uBuntu-botho, is deeply rooted in traditional culture, and has been widely supported as a precondition for the good functioning of contemporary democratic societies. Indeed, it was civilized dialogue in extremely difficult conditions that was the foundation of our peaceful constitutional revolution. The Constitution that emerged therefore presupposes that public power will be exercised in a manner that is not arbitrary and not unduly disrespectful of the dignity of those adversely affected by the exercise.[31]

Here we see how Justice Sachs appeals to civility and uBuntu-botho as principles that were part of the peaceful revolution. Sachs mobilizes these principles against a certain kind of violence that could possibly undermine the ethical integrity of the new constitutional institutions.[32]

For Justice Sachs, uBuntu-botho can and should also be used to create innovative remedies in the private law. In the *Dikoko* case, Justice Sachs wrote a concurring opinion agreeing with Justice Yvonne Mokgoro's advocacy that the ancient remedy of an *amende honorable* should be reinstated as a possible remedy in defamation cases. In Mokgoro's judgment, she found that the quantum of damages could potentially have an impact on the relationship between dignity and freedom of expression, and therefore excessive monetary awards could have a chilling effect on freedom of expression. As a result, the quantum of damages can be considered a constitutional issue. For Justice Sachs, however, and for Justice Mokgoro, the key issue in that case was actually to develop new remedies that do not turn on monetary awards, because such awards can actually have the effect of deepening the conflict between the parties.

Both Justice Mokgoro and Justice Sachs underscore that money is not even what the parties seek, and that it is a poor stand-in for a public apology, which could potentially restore the relation between the opposing parties. Justice Sachs argues:

> Although *uBuntu-botho* and the *amende honorable* are expressed in different languages intrinsic to separate legal cultures, they share the same underlying philosophy and goal. Both are directed towards promoting face-to-face encounter between the parties, so as to facilitate resolution in public of their differences and the restoration of harmony in the community. In both legal cultures the center-piece of the process is to create conditions to facilitate the achievement, if at all possible, of an apology honestly offered, and generously accepted.
>
> Thus, although I believe the actual award made by the High Court in this matter was way over the top, and accordingly associate myself with Mokgoro J's minority finding in this regard, my concern is not restricted to the excessiveness of the amount. It lies primarily with the fact that the law, as presently understood and applied, does far too little to encourage repair and reconciliation between the parties. In this respect the High Court cannot be faulted. The concerns expressed above were not raised in the papers or addressed in argument before it. The Court was simply working with a well-tried remedy in the ordinary way. Unfortunately, the hydraulic pressure on all concerned to go with the traditional legal flow inevitably produces a set of rules that are self-referential and self-perpetuating. The whole forensic mindset, as well as the way evidence is led and arguments are presented, is functionally and exclusively geared towards enlarging or restricting the amount of damages to be awarded, rather than towards securing an apology. In my view, this fixed concentration on quantum requires amendment. Greater scope has to be given for reparatory remedies.[33]

Sachs, with his useful flair, argues against the "hydraulic pressure" to impose monetary remedies in defamation cases. Neither Justice Mokgoro nor Justice Sachs simply argue against damages in all cases: in some cases damages would be necessary. But again, for Sachs, flexibility is demanded, because what is sought even within the private law is the creation of a more "civil" society, which is certainly a mandate of uBuntu-botho:

> What is needed, then, is more flexibility and innovation concerning the relation between apology and money awards. A good beginning for achieving greater remedial suppleness might well be to seek out the point of overlap between uBuntu-botho and the amende honorable, the first providing a new spirit, the second a time-honored legal format. Whatever renovatory modalities are employed, and however significant to the

outcome the facts will have to be in each particular case, the fuller the range of remedial options available the more likely will justice be done between the parties. And the greater the prospect of realizing the more human society envisaged by the Constitution.[34]

Equaliberty and uBuntu-botho: socio-economic and solidarity rights

When Sachs was in exile in Mozambique, he developed an expansive notion of rights, in response to a group of black law students at the University Natal-Durban in South Africa. The young black law students had come together in a group that called itself the Anti-Bill of Rights Committee. The argument of the Committee was that a Bill of Rights would become one more excuse for the reinforcement of privileges in a country where 87 percent of the land and 95 percent of the productive capital was owned by whites. Along classical revolutionary lines, the Committee held that the conventional liberal rights of a Bill of Rights would be a powerful tool for preventing the people's government from implementing radical economic measures to make equality into something more than an empty dream. In response, Sachs wrote a paper for the Constitutional Committee of the ANC, strongly defending the need for the ANC to set up an "anti-anti-Bill of Rights Committee." However, Sachs took the arguments of the young law students very seriously: he could see that a conventional, liberal Bill of Rights rooted in the rights of citizens as free persons might well be too narrow for the necessary egalitarian changes that would have to take place not only in South Africa, but in most African countries. We need to note here that these students were representing a strong Marxist heritage that critiques juridical forms as themselves inevitably bourgeois, and tied to capitalist relations of production.[35]

Sachs's solution was to argue that there is no reason why a Bill of Rights has to be limited to vertical application of the Constitution (the individual versus the state) or to rights rooted in fundamental liberties. To expand the concept of the Bill of Rights itself, Sachs developed the idea, proposed by the Czech jurist Karel Vasak in the late 1970s, that there are three "generations" of rights. The first generation encompassed those rights that emerged during the French and American revolutions, such as the right to free speech, the right to own property, the right to be free from unjustified searches and detention, etc. The second generation included rights that Sachs explicitly associated with revolutionary movements, including the Russian Revolution, which were ultimately entered into the South African Constitution as socio-economic rights. These included the right to health, the right to housing, the right to education, and the right to welfare. Importantly, these rights were given equal constitutional force as first generation rights, which are widely defended as the fundamentals of a liberal society. The third generation of rights by definition had to belong to communities rather than individuals, and included the right to solidarity and the rights to such shared goods as a clean environment, clean water, etc. Kader Asmal, a long-time member of Parliament, has referred to the three generations of rights as blue rights (civil and political), red rights (socio-economic), and green rights (human solidarity).

When the constitutional negotiations began, there were three separate positions on enforceability. Some argued that these rights were merely aspirational ideals, and could not be legally incorporated into a constitution. Others argued that these rights could be incorporated into the Constitution, but only if they had the status of guiding principles that would not be enforceable by the courts. The third position, defended by Sachs, was ultimately incorporated into the South African Constitution. Sachs explicitly argued that all three rights were necessary. He understood the worry that many of the so-called socialist states had often denied people's basic freedoms in the name of socio-economic policies. But for Sachs, the struggle itself had made these rights interdependent:

> Put crudely, there was a fear that in pursuit of the right to bread, the right to freedom would be submerged. Anxiety on this score had strong and unfortunate historical underpinning. Certain states had contended that in order to achieve national development and to improve the conditions of the impoverished masses, they had had to suppress freedom of speech, do away with multi-party democracy and spurn an open society. Could it be, though, that people wanted freedom without bread, or bread without freedom? In South Africa the struggle for the vote and for freedom of movement and speech, had always been inseparable from the fight for housing, health, and education. Bureaucratic authoritarianism had been intrinsic to apartheid; people simply did not count as human beings, hence the squalid housing and inferior education for the majority. The restoration of dignity for all South Africans accordingly required both the development of increased respect for the personality rights and freedom of each one of us and the creation of material conditions for a dignified life for all.[36]

One of the earliest cases concerning socio-economic rights to come before the Constitutional Court was the *Grootboom* case. Ms. Grootboom herself lived with her two children and her sister, and her sister's three children, in a shack near Cape Town. The winter rains were approaching, and she was determined not to live one more winter in a water-logged shack. About 5,000 people lived in similar circumstances in the same settlement. They had no electricity, no clean water, no sewage, no garbage removal. Many of the 5,000 or so people had applied to the municipality for subsidized low-cost housing, and had been put in a line. Some had been waiting for seven years or more. To avoid the brutality of the winter rains, Ms. Grootboom and close to a thousand others moved to a nearby vacant hillside. This hillside had in fact been designated as land to be used for low-cost housing. Negotiations with the owner and the local council failed. Ultimately, a court ordered an eviction, and they were removed. Houses were bulldozed, belongings destroyed. Of course, the images of forcible removals haunt the new South Africa, because it is integral to the country's brutal history. They had no choice but to move again, this time to a bare field with little more than plastic sheets for protection. Clearly, the council had long-term plans to build subsidized housing, but the burning question was: how long must people live and wait in intolerable conditions? Thus, it was in the *Grootboom* case that the Court was first confronted with how to give meaning to socio-economic rights, and the role of the Court in enforcing them. To quote Sachs:

> The right of access to adequate housing would have no meaning if a thousand people, in this case as a result of state action, were left without a place to lay their heads and without even minimal shelter, only a spot on a dusty ground and a few pieces of protective plastic sheeting. The problem facing us then was how to find a secure jurisprudential foundation for responding to their situation, that is, how to provide a principled analysis and remedy that would be consonant with our limited institutional capacity, and yet be capable of meaningful enforcement.[37]

The Constitutional Court, in unanimously adhering to a judgment written by Justice Zac Yacoob, further developed the concept in the Bill of Rights of "reasonable measures" that must be taken in order to progressively realize the right to housing. The notion of reasonableness, for the Court, was something that they could adjudicate, even if at the same time, they recognized that the Court would need careful analysis of the policy choices that might be consistent with this concept of reasonableness. In this case, even though subsidized low-cost housing was in the works, the local government had made no provision for the desperate situation of those entirely without a roof over their heads. In other words, even if the housing program could be judged reasonable in some long-range sense, it failed utterly to meet the actual horrifying conditions under which Ms. Grootboom and thousands of others were living. Thus, ultimately, the Court judged that the housing program was unreasonable, precisely because it did not make provision for desperate people with no shelter at all who were obviously in a terrible crisis situation. There had, in other words, to be some additional program developed for emergency provision of shelter.

The Court underscored that the right to dignity under section 10 of the Constitution was integrally connected to the right to housing. This understanding of socio-economic rights as integral to dignity takes us back to Sachs's work in Mozambique, as well as to Balibar's argument that equality and liberty are intrinsically intertwined, and that both sides of what he therefore calls "equaliberty" must be taken completely seriously. Sachs refuses the usual liberal solution of privileging liberty over equality, and instead always strives to articulate the complex relationship contained within the idea of equaliberty, which is also contained within the South African Constitution. Intertwining liberty and equality is of course difficult, given the division of powers which is embodied in the South African Constitution, between the role of the judiciary and the role of the legislature. Thus, the Court's judgment did not include anything like an actual program to close the gap: this was left open to other branches of the government to decide, including on the question of whether any local program would be sufficient, or whether it would have to be a national program. In a like manner, other branches of the government were given great flexibility on how they were to raise the money for such an emergency program. But for all the flexibility given to other branches of the government in the development of the plan, the judgment made it clear that some kind of formulaic program of subsidized housing was not enough. The beauty of the Court's decision lies in its recognition that the desperate situation of the totally homeless is a form of violence that can undermine an individual human being's dignity to the point that it makes a mockery of the very ideal of dignity, which in the South African Constitution is both an ideal, a moral attribution to persons, and an actually enforceable right. As Sachs writes:

> We accordingly made it plain that the right of access to housing could not be separated from the right to human dignity. This meant that a purely quantitative response by the state to its obligations would not be enough, even if by international standards it made extraordinary provision for access to formal housing. The qualitative dimension could never be forgotten.[38]

At stake here, of course, is the big question of how far the Court can and should go in the actualization of socio-economic rights. I stand with those critics who argue that the Court has not gone far enough, and I will return to that argument shortly. But it is important to stress here that what the Court *has* done is change the narration in which squatters were plainly seen — as they are in the United States — as people who are simply stealing land from someone who has the absolute right to own it, and therefore to force others off their land. Whatever one makes of the Court's successes in the realm of socio-economic rights, this change of narration is itself hugely significant, in that there are now human beings on both sides of the conflict whose dignity must be respected.[39]

In the *Grootboom* case, the Court was not faced with ordering an eviction or upholding an order for eviction, because the thousand or so people involved in the case had already been evicted and had their homes brutally destroyed. The central issue, then, was emergency shelter. But in the *Port Elizabeth* case, the Constitutional Court was confronted with whether or not to uphold an order of eviction. As we have seen, the *Grootboom* case turned to both the moral ideal and the legal right of dignity to underscore what was constitutionally at stake, and in this case Sachs signed on to the unanimous judgment that did not appeal to uBuntu-botho. But when he was confronted in *Port Elizabeth* with upholding an order of eviction, he did use uBuntu-botho.

Section 25 of the Constitution upholds the right to property; section 26 establishes housing rights. I want to argue that uBuntu-botho is not a secondary ideal in this judgment, but is central to the judicial reasoning about the question of how and when evictions can be ordered. Sachs, in his judicial autobiography, explains that, for better or worse, most of the cases with which he has dealt in the Constitutional Court were between right and right, and the question was how to put these rights together in some kind of meaningful form. This conflict comes up in part because of how seriously the South African Constitution takes the idea of equaliberty, and therefore is confronted with many of the seeming aporias presented by the attempt to institutionalize equaliberty. Yet of course a judge is not a philosopher who can simply point to the difficulties or even the aporias and then quit his or her business. A judge, by his or her position on the Constitutional Court, must judge and therefore seek coherent solutions at the level of constitutional law for competing right situations which are unavoidable if the state or the Constitutional Court seeks to institutionalize equaliberty. Sachs's insistence that sections 25 and 26 of the Constitution must be read together effectively turns the right to property away from the notion that if one owns a piece of property, one has the right of total possession to it. This reading of the two rights together moves us close to a thorough revaluation of what the universal right to property is within the conception of "equaliberty." Étienne Balibar has argued that:

> The real content of the universal property of nature is nothing but a *universal politics* of mediation of the interests and ends of public and private property. And more and more it appears that it cannot be enacted by unilateral or authoritarian means. It at least potentially includes a new political practice, democracy's crossing of a frontier (and of many borders), since it cannot exist without the participation or contribution of *all* "proprietors," even the poorest and most oppressed.[40]

To understand how this revaluation is given legal content in Justice Sachs's judgment, we need to look at how he interprets section 26(3) of the Constitution, imposing a specific obligation on the courts to grapple with all the complexity of the competing rights involved in a conflict such as the one over eviction, to bring about as much reconciliation as possible between the two opposing sides. To quote Justice Sachs:

> In sum, the Constitution imposes new obligations on the courts concerning rights relating to property not previously recognized by the common law. It counterposes to the normal ownership rights of possession, use and occupation, a new and equally relevant right not arbitrarily to be deprived of a home. The expectations that ordinarily go with title could clash head-on with the genuine despair of people in dire need of accommodation. The judicial function in these circumstances is not to establish a hierarchical arrangement between the different interests involved, privileging in an abstract and mechanical way the rights of ownership over the right not to be dispossessed of a home, or vice versa. Rather it is to balance out and reconcile the opposed claims in as just a manner as possible taking account of all the interests involved and the specific factors relevant in each particular case.[41]

Next, Sachs offers an uBuntu-related reading of the Prevention of Illegal Eviction from and Unlawful Occupation of Land Act 19 of 1998 (PIE). For Sachs, an interpretation of PIE must begin with an extensive contextual analysis of the circumstances of any particular occupation of land. For example, it is necessary to consider how long the occupiers have been on the land; what kind of communities they have formed; where their children go to school; what job possibilities have been made available because of where they live; etc. He then carefully analyzes how one should interpret the "availability" or "suitable alternative accommodation" of land, which is discussed in section 6(3) of PIE. Here we see Justice Sachs echoing the concern of the Court in *Grootboom* that a long-range plan for subsidized housing may not be enough, indeed *will* not be enough if those who are most desperate are ignored. Thus, the courts must look at the actual situation of those who are squatting, and this is part and parcel of how competing rights situations must be addressed. It is not enough for the Court to simply weigh the rights or the language of the statute through the more commonly recognized notions of statutory interpretation:

> The obligation on the court is to "have regard to" the circumstances, that is, to give them due weight in making its judgment as to what is just and equitable. The court cannot fulfil its responsibilities in this respect if it does not have the requisite information at its disposal. It needs to be fully apprised of the circumstances before it can have regard to them. It follows that although it is incumbent on the interested parties to make all relevant information available, technical questions relating to onus of proof should not play an unduly significant role in its enquiry. The court is not resolving a civil dispute as to who has rights under land law; the existence of unlawfulness is the foundation for the enquiry, not its subject matter.[42]

Sachs argues that anything like a just and equitable solution cannot be achieved unless the Court goes beyond what some would see at its appropriate function, to create a hierarchy of rules that define rights and engage with a deep and profound examination of the actual conditions of the occupiers. Again, to quote Sachs:

> Thus, PIE expressly requires the court to infuse elements of grace and compassion into the formal structures of law. It is called upon to balance competing interests in a principled way and to promote the constitutional vision of a caring society based on good neighborliness and shared concern. The Constitution and PIE confirm that we are not islands unto ourselves. The spirit of *uBuntu*, part of the deep cultural heritage of the majority of the population, suffuses the whole constitutional order. It combines individual rights with a communitarian philosophy. It is a unifying motif of the Bill of Rights, which is nothing if not a structured, institutionalised and operational declaration in our evolving society of the need for human interdependence, respect and concern.[43]

In the above quote, Sachs argues that uBuntu is a unifying motive of the Bill of Rights, and that it is also a justiciable principle. Indeed, I want to suggest that uBuntu-botho structures the judgment's entire analysis of the relationship between sections 25 (the right to property) and 26 (the right to housing) and the relation of the Constitution to PIE, and that it also constitutes the basis for the development of a complex notion of judicial obligation in the context of evictions. The role of mediation is not simply a way to save money in Sachs's judgment: it is crucial to bringing people into a face-to-face relationship, where those who own the land actually have to face those who have squatted, as human beings, not disposable objects that are in the way of their right to property. This insistence on face-to-face engagement is crucial in Sachs's legal development of uBuntu-botho as crucial to the interpretation of what might be a just and equitable situation in any given context in which sections 25 and 26 come into conflict. In order for a genuine reconciliation through uBuntu-botho to take place, or even something that aspires to it, a first step is that human beings meet face-to-face and hear each other out. Thus, uBuntu-botho not only operationalizes certain obligations on the part of the judiciary: it imposes obligations on the opposing parties to respect that their conflicts are conflicts between human beings, which frequently involve extreme discrepancies in wealth. Mediation, then, is part of imposing obligations on the opposing parties, to confront one another and to do the best they can to work out an equitable situation between them.

In *Residents of Joe Slovo Community*, Sachs, in a concurring opinion, is one of the justices who found that the squatters were legitimately on the land in which they had built up a community over years. Some commentators have questioned whether Sachs's ultimate judgment that an eviction could be ordered due to the provision of low-cost housing, and the benefits that would accrue to the squatters in that housing, might be inconsistent with *Port Elizabeth*. I, too, have some questions to that effect. It is clear that the general thrust of Sachs's overall argument, although perhaps not his conclusion, follows the complex jurisprudence of eviction he developed under uBuntu-botho in *Port Elizabeth*. But I want to emphasize another aspect of that judgment, in which Sachs, in a highly original manner, connects "moral citizenship," or what Hannah Arendt famously designated as the "right to have rights,"[44] with the right to occupy land. We have already seen that Sachs has moved very close to Balibar in arguing that the right to property, both philosophically and certainly under the South African Constitution, cannot be read as a Common Law right of absolute possession. But what he is stressing here, in connecting occupation with moral citizenship, is that we may need to have a new way, an African way of thinking about occupation, given how disinheritance from the land was part and parcel of the denial of the humanity of those who were previously its occupants. Thus, it is not, for Sachs, just a question of the right to housing, but of a right to have rights that is at stake in these eviction cases, which is why there may be no more important cases in the new constitutional dispensation, because they connect dispossession of land with dispossession of humanity. To quote Sachs:

> [354] The first step taken by the Council in relation to its obligations to promote the right of the homeless to have access to adequate housing was to enable homeless families to occupy vacant land which it owned at the side of the N2 highway. To have refused the families the right to erect their temporary shelters on that land would have been manifestly unreasonable. For people in desperate quest of some place on earth to lay their heads, the erection of rudimentary structures on land from which they would not be expelled represented more than just establishing a shelter from the elements. Their simple habitations on council land gave them a zone of personal intimacy and family security, and established relatively inviolable spaces of privacy and tranquility in a turbulent and hostile world. Moreover, individuals who would otherwise have lived in insecure isolation became part of a community, with all the social interaction and organized facilities that living within a settled neighborhood provides. They escaped the status of pariahs who had been historically converted by colonial domination and racist laws into eternal wanderers in the land of their birth.[45]

Sachs then continues to quote Sol Plaatje in a footnote:

> The spiritual dimension of eviction and homelessness was captured with rare eloquence by Sol Plaatje in his famous book *Native Life in South Africa*

> (PS King & Son, Ltd. London 1916), recently re-published by Pan Macmillan South Africa, 2007. Referring to the effects of dispossession and homelessness created by the Native Land Act, 1913, he writes:
>
> "Awakening on Friday morning, June 20, 1913, the South African native found himself, not actually a slave, but a pariah in the land of his birth." (At 21.)
>
> "Mrs Kgobadi carried a sick baby when the eviction took place, and she had to transfer her darling from the cottage to the jolting ox-wagon in which they left the farm. Two days out the little one began to sink as the result of privation and exposure on the road, and the night before we met them its little soul was released from its earthly bonds. The death of the child added a fresh perplexity to the stricken parents. They had no right or title to the farmlands through which they trekked: they must keep to the public roads — the only places in the country open to the outcasts if they are possessed of travelling permit. The deceased child had to be buried, but where, when and how? This young wandering family decided to dig a grave under cover of the darkness of that night, when no-one was looking and in that crude manner the dead child was interred — and interred amid fear and trembling, as well as the throbs of a torturing anguish, in a stolen grave, lest the proprietor of the spot, or any of his servants, should surprise them in the act. Even criminals dropping straight from the gallows have an undisputed claim to six feet of ground on which to rest their criminal remains, but under the cruel operation of the Natives' Land Act little children, whose only crime is that God did not make them white, are sometimes denied that right in their ancestral home." (At 73–4.)

After quoting several other passages from Sol Plaatje, Sachs concludes the footnote:

> . . . Eight decades after these words were written, intervention came, not from outside, but in the form of our Constitution. It declares in its Preamble that South Africa belongs to all who live in it. This case is as much about access to full moral citizenship as it is about access to adequate housing.[46]

Sachs himself has recognized and taken seriously arguments that the Court should go further in actually curtailing the worst abuses of neoliberal capitalism, even if not taking over the role of the Parliament in developing actual programs for socio-economic rights. Still, we could ask whether uBuntu-botho itself might push towards a more socialist-oriented society, as many of the movements on the ground have argued. Thus, in a sense, uBuntu-botho could for instance be deployed so as to at least question whether or not an appeal to limited resources was legitimate, if the source of that limitation was unfettered market relationships, which even under Hegel would undermine the reach of the *Rechtsstaat*.[47]

Of course, I am well aware that uBuntu-botho has also been used to justify hierarchies. But like all ideals and values, it should be understood as part of a twofold struggle. The first is to insist that the constitutional project be Africanized by incorporating important ideals such as uBuntu-botho, even if these ideals do not justify themselves in their rootedness in an indigenous people, but as a universal project that should be heeded. The second is that the way of thinking about the relatedness of persons as an ethical one that inheres in uBuntu-botho can and has been mobilized to challenge neoliberal capitalist relations as not only inherent in the means of production, but in day-to-day life. In other words, uBuntu-botho, because it has an aspirational edge, is not something that is just there to be discovered: it is itself a matter of struggle, and many on-the-ground movements have evoked uBuntu-botho in their continuing demand, not only for a future socialist society, but for different ways of living together within the movements themselves. On a broader scale, it could certainly be argued that the limit on socio-economic rights, which inheres in the phrase that the state mandate is always within the limits of "available resources, to achieve the progressive realization of each of these rights," assumes as a natural necessity that there is some kind of inherent scarcity that could stand in the way of the realization of these rights. But of course, many Marxist economists have argued that the scarcity is the result of neoliberal capitalism, and that human beings are responsible for the limitation of resources.[48] The question then becomes: can the evocation of uBuntu-botho be used to challenge this so-called necessity in the name of an ethical way of being together that would demand that there be much greater equality, not only in terms of distribution of goods, but in the more traditional socialist sense, of access to the means of production themselves?

The postcolonial *Rechtsstaat*: Hegel and Kant in South Africa

I have argued that the South African Constitutional Court has developed a *Rechtsstaat* that is complex, because some of Hegel's presuppositions about a *Rechtsstaat* cannot apply in a post-colony. First of all, in a country like South Africa, with many ethnic affiliations, languages, and intellectual heritages, there cannot be the kind of denaturing of identity in the sense meant by Hegel. In Hegel, one of the hallmarks of European modernity was precisely to legally underscore personhood, so that former, more "traditional" modes of belonging were undermined, to be replaced with a process of identification and disidentification with all fields of endeavor possible in modern life. This notion of a person, free to have multiple identifications, lies at the heart of Hegel's notion of freedom. Given the symbolic violence imposed by apartheid on the intellectual heritages of the majority population, such a process, which is certainly recognized in the South African Constitution and jurisprudence on dignity and subjective freedom, still must be ethically limited by a profound respect for those intellectual heritages that were disregarded, or even worse, condemned as barbaric. In like manner, then, South Africa cannot be the kind of national community envisioned by Hegel, precisely because it must grapple with the colonial legacy and with the claims upon the government of deep and profound respect for the rich legacies of the majority of the population, which include recognition of divergent sources of law, such as the living customary law.

We have seen that Sachs, in an innovative judgment, develops the notion of the reasonable new South African. Any country that seeks to institutionalize the great ideals such as dignity and uBuntu-botho inevitably "normalizes," in that it aims to create standards which citizens are called both to aspire to and to seek to incorporate in their day-to-day lives.[49] I put "normalizes" in quotation marks because the very idea of a *Rechtsstaat*, which is to normatively guide civil society and limit it in an overarching ethical scheme, inevitably sets up normative standards, both for legal persons and for citizens. It is precisely because the *Rechtsstaat* seeks to normatively regulate civil society, or what has come to be known in Europe and Anglo-American thinking as civil society — Marx, of course, would find nothing "civil" about the brutal relations imposed by advanced capitalism — that it creates ethical mandates which have the effect, because they are normative, of normalization. The Marxist critique was that the Hegelian *Rechtsstaat* failed to recognize that the normative regulation of "civil society" not only normalized but legitimated exploitation. We have already seen that the South African Constitution goes considerably further than most liberal constitutions in its attempt to implement equaliberty through socio-economic rights. Whether it has gone far enough, given the brutal reality of neoliberal capitalism, is of course a burning question. But for my purposes here, I simply want to underscore that the institutionalization of ideals in the form of rights, such as the classic example of dignity in the South African Constitution, does create standards that regulate day-to-day relationships. Direct horizontal application takes that regulation one step further, in that what would often be thought of as spheres of privacy are also subject to constitutional regulation and thus regulation by the constitutional ideals. This normalization is not in and of itself negative, although it can have a negative side, and can carry within it all the problems of any appeal to ideals, which is that by the very process of idealization, there are exclusions that follow from it. What of course is key is precisely the appeal to values and ideals as the framework through which rights must be both interpreted and combined. Sachs makes this explicit in *Sidumo and Another* v. *Rustenburg Platinum Mines*:

> [148] Acceptance of hybridity is based on the fact that protected rights in a constitutional democracy overlap, intersect and mutually reinforce

each other. Though in particular factual situations the interests secured by the rights might collide, there can be no intrinsic or categorical incompatibility between the rights themselves. Courts should not feel obliged to obliterate one right through establishing the categorical or classificatory pre-eminence of another. On the contrary, the task of the courts is to seek wherever possible to balance and reconcile the constitutional interests involved. In this endeavor the courts will be strongly guided by the constitutional values at stake.

[149] The values of the Constitution are strong, explicit and clearly intended to be considered part of the very texture of the constitutional project. They are implicit in the very structure and design of the new democratic order. The letter and the spirit of the Constitution cannot be separated; just as the values are not free-floating, ready to alight as mere adornments on this or that provision, so is the text not self-supporting, awaiting occasional evocative enhancement. The role of constitutional values is certainly not simply to provide a patina of virtue to otherwise bald, neutral and discrete legal propositions. Text and values work together in integral fashion to provide the protections promised by the Constitution. And by their nature, values resist compartmentalization.[50]

The very idea of a *Rechtsstaat* implies this kind of integration, but it does so in a way that frames the legal issues at stake in a way that is quite foreign to Anglo-American law. In Anglo-American law, there is a distinction between law, morality, and ethics. But in critical idealism from Kant on, law *is* morality, as the realm of external freedom. Thus, the framework, as we have seen in South Africa, of legal interpretation always takes the Court back to its fundamental task of giving actuality to the great ideals of the substantive revolution, which are embodied in the Constitution.

In his carefully crafted judgment dealing with the rights of unmarried cohabitants, *Volks NO* v. *Robinson and Others*, Sachs reminds us that the legal landscape of the substantive revolution in South Africa is not the limited one of so-called legal rules or black letter law.[51] It has to be referred back to the entirety of the spirit of the Constitution, in the strong Hegelian sense of the word "spirit":

[152] In my view, the question of the fairness of excluding such survivors from such benefits falls to be assessed not in the narrow confines of the rules established by matrimonial law, but rather within the broader and more situation-sensitive framework of the principles of family law, principles that are evolving rapidly in our new constitutional era. By its very nature, the quality of fairness, like that of mercy and justice, is not strained. The enquiry as to what is fair in our new constitutional democracy accordingly does not pass easily through the eye of the needle of black-letter law. Judicial dispassion does not exclude judicial

> compassion; the question of fairness must be rigorously dealt with, but in a people-centered and not a rule-centered way.[52]

Sachs's understanding that the legal landscape of a substantive revolution must be explicitly rooted in the values and ideals that are themselves the basis of rights does not, of course, deny in any way the importance of the interpretation of the enumerated rights themselves. But how that enumeration is to take place is precisely what demands a new legal landscape. Sachs writes in *Sidumo*:

> [150] The Bill of Rights does specifically identify a number of rights for special constitutional protection. Each is independently delineated, reflecting historical experience pointing to the need to be on guard in areas of special potential vulnerability and abuse. Each has produced an outgrowth of specialist legal learning. Yet enumerating themes for dedicated attention does not presuppose or permit detaching the listed rights from the foundational values that nurture them. Nor does it justify severing the rights from the underlying values that give substance and texture to the Constitution as a whole. On the contrary, in a value-based constitutional democracy with a normative structure that is seamless, organic and ever-evolving, the manner in which claims to constitutional justice are typified and dealt with, should always be integrated within the context of the setting, interests and values involved.[53]

The *Rechtsstaat*, then, even as it has to be reconceived in the course of a postcolonial constitution, still pulls us to shared ideals as part of the new ethical order, and this is unavoidable. And with caution: all to the good. But to recognize the inevitability of normalization in a *Rechtsstaat* is not to reject the idea of a *Rechtsstaat*, but instead to be sensitive to some of the dangers inherent in ideality.[54]

As a Justice, Sachs has been particularly conscientious in his efforts to counterbalance the inevitable normalization that is part of any *Rechtsstaat* with a deep and profound sensitivity to difference, particularly in groups that are marginalized, and thus opened either to suspicion or, worse yet, contempt. In the *Prince* case, a young man was denied the right to become a lawyer, because he was part of the Rastafarian religion, and therefore used cannabis for ritual purposes. The young man sought an exemption, which was not recreational, but part and parcel of religious expression. The majority found that it was simply too hard to try to create such an exception, because it would be very difficult to enforce. Sachs, in his dissent, argued that it is precisely groups like the Rastafarians that need protection, both for historical reasons and because of their inability to exercise effective power to protect themselves through legislation. Rastafarianism, which is only a relatively small religion in South Africa, has been associated with anti-colonial movements, so there are historical reasons for Sachs to recognize the unique status of Rastafarianism in South Africa. In this case, we not only see Sachs's sensitivity to the historical and symbolic violence done to an intellectual heritage such as the Rastafarians, but we also begin to engage with his rich notion of what it means for a judge to judge.

> In my view the majority judgment puts a thumb on the scales in favor of ease of law enforcement, and gives insufficient weight to the impact the measure will have, not only on the fundamental rights of the appellant and his religious community, but on the basic notion of tolerance and respect for diversity that our Constitution demands for and from all in our society.
>
> The weighing of the respective interests at stake does not take place on weightless scales of pure logic pivoted on a friction-free fulcrum of abstract rationality. The balancing has to be done in the context of a lived and experienced historical, sociological and imaginative reality. Even if for purposes of making its judgment the Court is obliged to classify issues in conceptual terms and abstract itself from such reality, it functions with materials drawn from that reality and has to take account of the impact of its judgments on persons living within that reality. Moreover, the Court itself is part of that reality and must engage in a complex process of simultaneously detaching itself from and engaging with it. I believe that in the present matter, history, imagination and mind-set play a particularly significant role, especially with regard to the weight to be given to the various factors in the scales.[55]

Sachs has been utterly honest in his description of how he judges. As we see in the above quote, he underscores the importance of the imagination. He describes how some of his most profound insights came to him while in a bath, in a semi-conscious state. Thus, the role of intuition is crucial for Sachs, in how a judge discovers what might be the right decision in a particular case. Sachs distinguishes between discovery, justification, and persuasion in the actual process of judging. Given his emphasis on intuition and imagination, it is not surprising that Sachs also wants to guard against what he sees as too much subjectivity. The role of the limitations imposed by the ideals of the *Rechtsstaat*, as well as the legal community to which one belongs, clearly plays a role for Sachs, and we will turn to the role of the community shortly.

To bring out the significance of the fact that what a judge does is judge, Sachs turns to Jennifer Nedelsky's reading of Hannah Arendt's lectures on Kant's writings on the power of judgment. Although both Nedelsky and Arendt misunderstand Immanuel Kant's notion of the *sensus communis*, in that they confuse the ideality of this community with an actual community, Kant's notion of how one reflects on one's own judgments of taste is relevant to Sachs's concept of judging. What Nedelsky and Arendt get wrong is that Kant's community of taste is a "community of the should-be," not an actual community. Judgments of taste in Kant are both subjective and universal, which of course seems like a paradox. For those unfamiliar with Kant's critical philosophy, let me dare to provide a brief summary of how this informs his analysis of judgments of taste.

For Kant, our reason, as finite creatures, must operate in such a way that it gives us a knowable world of scientific law. In science, we make determinate judgments by applying the categories of the understanding to reality, and these judgments are true or false in the sense that they are open to truth-based validity claims. Sachs himself clearly distinguishes between truth in science and what he calls "dialogical truth," which arises in the courts in debates about particular cases. In science, the imagination, which is productive in Kant, not passive, as in Hume, is still entirely in the service of the understanding. Without intuition or imagination in Kant, there would be no world of objects to which we apply the categories of the understanding. But in judgments of taste, it is the free play of the imagination working in association with the understanding, not subordinated to it, which gives us the subjective feeling of pleasure upon which a subjective judgment such as, "This is a beautiful rose," is based.

The difficulty here is that these judgments are both subjective and universal. The key is to grasp that our human reason and imagination must operate the same way in each one of us as finite creatures. Therefore, given the universalizability of our faculties, if I have the experience of the pleasure of the free play of the understanding and the imagination, so should you, as a creature who must — and I underscore the word "must" — cognize the world in a particular way. But the "should" is also crucial here: when I call upon you to join in my judgment, I am appealing to a "community of the should-be," not an actual community that exists, and thus in the course of the judgment, an ideal community is at least configured that did not necessarily exist before. To quote Kant:

> Now this happens by one holding his judgment up not so much to the actual as to the merely possible judgments of others, and putting himself into the position of everyone else, merely by abstracting from the limitations that contingently attach to our own judging; which is in turn accomplished by leaving out as far as is possible everything in one's representational state that is matter, i.e., sensation, and attending solely to the formal peculiarities of his representation or his representational state.[56]

But how does one reflect on one's own judgment? Kant gives us three principles of reflection: to think for oneself; to try to think in the position of everyone else (which Sachs, following Arendt, calls the "enlarged mentality");

and to think consistently, or in accordance with oneself. But these are principles for reflection on judgment, not an appeal to the conventions of an actually existing community.

The importance of getting Kant right is not only scholarly, and is particularly relevant to South Africa. There is a profound sense in which the substantive revolution involves what Emeritus Justice Laurie Ackermann has referred to as moral, not just constitutional mandates.[57] In a very important sense, then, the judgments of the Constitutional Court are calling a "community of the should-be" into being, in that the entire ethical and moral fabric of society has to be revolutionized in accordance with the ideals of the Constitution. Even when Sachs appeals to a democratic society rooted in freedom, dignity, and equality, he explicitly recognizes that this appeal is to an ideal. As he writes:

> Such a society is a notional one. It is not to be found in this country or that. It does not have this particular constitution or that, this kind of judiciary or that. It is an ideal type of society, constructed out of the actual experience of the way issues of power and of rights are dealt with in countries that are widely regarded as democratic . . . This imagined society then becomes the template for measuring the constitutionality of governmental laws and conduct. Reference to the qualities of such a society frequently tips the scales in the borderline cases that typically reach us.[58]

Indeed, Sachs emphasizes how the legal community itself must evolve in accordance with the Constitution, and therefore I would argue that the understanding of the *sensus communis* as a "community of the should-be" is precisely what puts a moral mandate on the existing legal community to change in accordance with the new constitutional dispensation. It is important to note that section 7(1) of the Constitution, which promotes a society rooted in democracy, freedom, dignity, and equality, can best be understood both as a constitutional mandate and as a regulative ideal. It is a regulative ideal in the sense that Immanuel Kant defended the necessity for a critical notion of telos to configure the great ideals that always escape full embodiment. In the case of South Africa, as we have seen, this critical telos is often expressed in a bridge metaphor rooted in transformation, in which the new South Africa is to transform the institutions of injustice under apartheid into a new dispensation worthy of the substantive revolution. In Kant, telos is a critical notion, precisely because it can never be philosophically demonstrated. But as a constitutional mandate, under section 7(1), the move to realize the great ideals embodied in the Bill of Rights is always towards a new society. Thus, the "new" in the phrase, "new South Africa," points precisely to this critical telos.

Of course, to think from the standpoint of an "enlarged mentality" does not have to be an abstract exercise. Instead, one can well imagine the dialogic partners with whom a judge is actually engaging as he or she struggles with a particular decision. In that sense, the actual community in which one finds oneself can play a role in the imaginative exercise by which one principally tries to delimit what Sachs calls the idiosyncratic individualized nature of the discovery. There is a sense, then, in which dialogic truth imagines the interlocutors to whom one is immediately responsible. To quote Sachs:

> So when I follow my legal conscience and articulate a judgment in a particular way, I think immediately of my colleagues on the Court who will be reading it, and console myself with the thought that if I do not persuade them this time round, perhaps I am planting the seed of a new approach by them in future cases. I imagine judges and magistrates in other courts, wrestling with their own judgments, reading it and possibly getting assistance from it. I think of legal practitioners pouncing on it in search of arguments to assist their clients. Having been a law teacher for many years, I envisage academics propelling their critical ploughs through it, discussing it with their students, and possibly using it as a footnote in their textbooks. And especially I think of students engaging with it, their minds still questing, their idealism alive. What can the law do for ordinary people? What language should the law use to express itself in accessible and persuasive form?[59]

As Sachs argues, respect is built into this process of deliberation. This respect underscores what he refers to as the institutional modesty of the judge. This institutional modesty is that one is not trying to get the upper hand over colleagues to which one is in disagreement. If there is disagreement on the bench, then one of course does have to take into account that it is possible to be wrong. A part of the imaginative exercise, as Sachs reminds us, is not to pretend to be Hercules, whom Ronald Dworkin figures as a judge who is able to rise above the to-and-fro of actual debate and make the right decision.[60] Instead, the appeal to imagined interlocutors in the course of judging not only implies a dialogical view of truth: it also insists on the individual judge's voice as one voice among many. Kant's principles of reflecting upon a reflective judgment certainly help to promote the kind of honesty of voice to which Sachs always strives. For Sachs, this respect for interlocutors not only includes respect for one's colleagues on the Court, but also respect for the different branches of government, and therefore, for Sachs at least, the interlocutors, which he imagines are not simply those of the legal community and in the judiciary, but also those in other branches of government. Here, again, Sachs returns to his notion of civility:

> Civility in public life goes well beyond good manners. It is an element that favors democratic pluralism . . . Accordingly, civility is explicitly required in the relations between the three branches of government

> themselves. Indeed, a dialogic relation between judiciary and government is inherent to the very structure of our Constitution. Our Court has extensive powers of judicial review, including the competence to declare an Act of Parliament invalid to the extent that it is inconsistent with the Constitution. This means that we are constantly dealing with challenges to the validity of legislation. The powers granted to our Court in this respect are great. When declaring a statute to be unconstitutional and invalid, we may make any order that is just and equitable, including one giving Parliament a grace period within which to correct the defect in the law. The notion of a dialogue or conversation with Parliament is therefore built into the very determination of our jurisdiction. And in my more vain moments I imagine that when they are considering how to draft a new law, members of Parliament will read what Sachs J had to say on a particular problem, or at least that their law advisors will glance at selected passages or summaries.[61]

So, as we see, Sachs takes very seriously the idea to be as inclusive as possible of the standpoint of others, even while at times recognizing that one must dare to be a lone voice. Without this daring, the actual legal community would not be challenged, and this challenge is obviously crucially important in the new South Africa, where many members of the judiciary and the legal system were trained in the old order:

> Indeed, part of the extraordinary intensity of being a judge on the Constitutional Court has flowed from the knowledge that as a new court applying a new constitution it had constantly to be re-defining the norms and standards of judicial reasoning. Furthermore, it had to do so in a way that simultaneously destabilized the legal community by introducing change, and reinforced the community's self-assurance by justifying in a principled way the forward movement. In this regard I believe it is particularly important that when we re-arrange elements that the legal community has long regarded as virtually axiomatic, we explain precisely what we are doing in the most open and transparent way possible.[62]

Here we are again returned to the "should-be" of the *sensus communis*, in which a changed community is brought into existence through the judgments themselves. But, of course, part of the role of the judge is to persuade the legal community that the judgment is acceptable, and in that sense one must take account of actually existing communities that one is seeking to persuade. Thus, in a sense, even judgments that seem daring because they do demand changes in the status quo, at times even of how law is conceived by the status quo, must still seek to persuade through an interpretation of the legal meaning of the new constitutional order. As Sachs reminds us: "In particular, a judgment that bases itself on introducing radical changes to the principles and standards hitherto firmly accepted by the legal community would have to set out persuasive references to the impact the new constitutional order has on re-defining the way the problem has to be looked at."[63]

But we need to emphasize yet another aspect of Sachs's insistence on dialogic truth. In the *Matatiele* case, the question was raised as to what branch of government was responsible for the shifting of provincial boundaries. For Sachs, it is never just a question of making a simple determination of which branch has which power, particularly in an area as delicate as that of drawing boundaries. Of course, as he recognizes in his concurring opinion, Parliament has itself set up procedures and a political body to handle this obviously volatile issue. But, for Sachs, the deeper problem had to do with the failure of the government of Kwazulu-Natal to provide adequate information. He emphasized that there could not be a constitution rooted in, and supportive of democratic participation in all aspects of law-making, unless adequate information, and perhaps even more importantly, candor, is shown on the part of all branches of government, including legislatures in the provinces. To quote Sachs:

> [109] The notion that "government knows best, end of enquiry", might have satisfied Justice Stratford CJ in the pre-democratic era. It is no longer compatible with democratic government based on the rule of law as envisaged by our Constitution. This Court has frequently acknowledged the wide legislative mandate given by the Constitution to Parliament. Democratically elected by the nation, Parliament is the engine-house of our democracy. One cannot but be mindful of the intense time-tabling pressures to which it is subjected in a period of institution-building and transformation. Yet the more significant the work that Parliament undertakes and the greater the pressures under which it operates, the stronger the need for government to provide an explanation for the introduction of legislation; robustness need not be equated with opaqueness.
>
> [110] As this case demonstrates, far from the foundational values of the rule of law and of accountable government existing in discreet categories, they overlap and reinforce each other. Openness of government promotes both the rationality that the rule of law requires, and the accountability that multi-party democracy demands. In our constitutional order, the legitimacy of laws made by Parliament comes not from awe, but from openness.[64]

The importance of Sachs's concurrence cannot be overemphasized. Often, constitutionalism is understood as a limit to democracy, and more specifically, a limit on the rule of the majority over minorities unable to wield power in the political arena. As we have seen, Sachs is extremely sensitive to how minorities can be subjected to discrimination, given the normalizing force of a *Rechtsstaat*. We saw his deep concern to protect those whose practices seem at odds even with the law in the *Prince* case. But here we see an important shift, not only for South African constitutional law, but for political theory. For Sachs, the very notion of a constitution rooted in values, one of which is democracy, is that the Court must itself promote conditions of dialogic encounter. This is impossible without openness and candor, because those values are crucial to any meaningful debate which allows all sides to understand the issues at stake. South Africa, of course, is a parliamentary democracy, where the issue of majority rule is not as heavily weighted as it is in the United States under the two-party system, where the winner takes all. Minority parties are represented in Parliament. Still, it is crucial, for Sachs, that the Constitution promote democracy as a value that is as important as the other great values of freedom and equality.

Conclusion: the idealist

Étienne Balibar has powerfully argued that a crucial component of the ethical crisis in Europe is the drying up of ideals for which young people are so thirsty, so that they often seek out symbols of idealization that either have lost their meaning or point to a rebellion that has nowhere to go. I am in complete agreement with him.[65] There is a profound sense in which Sachs himself has become an exemplar of the figure of the idealist. As we have seen, he was a freedom fighter from a young age, and even enduring torture, exile, and an assassination attempt did not turn him away from his commitments to revolutionary change in South Africa. He was, as we have seen, even an idealist in an armed struggle, seemingly the most non-ideal of situations, and he has remained an idealist in the best sense of the word as a constitutional judge.

Writing on Sachs has been a difficult undertaking because he has been one of my heroes, due to his unwavering idealism. In his movie, *The Flags of Our Fathers*, Clint Eastwood ends by questioning a certain kind of masculine heroism.[66] I am very aware of the dangers inherent in masculine heroism. It is Sachs's idealism, however, that makes him exceptional, as well as his searing honesty about what he has endured, and how he has felt about it. Thus, his is not the heroism of the man who braves everything and remains untouched by it: far from it. Indeed, one of the chapters of his book is called, "The Judge Who Cried":

> The courtroom has been packed with people wearing T-shirts saying "HIV Positive". There had been complete silence as we had handed down judgment. Then moments later when we had gone out to the passage at the back, I had heard cheering, and had found myself suddenly with tears in my eyes. It had not just been because of emotion about the impact of AIDS upon our country. The tears had come because of an overwhelming

> sense of pride at being a member of a court that protected fundamental rights and secured dignity for all.[67]

As Sachs notes, his tears were in part tears of pride of being a member of a Court that has taken on the daunting task of institutionalizing the ideals of the South African Constitution. Whatever one may make of the first 15 years of constitutional law in South Africa, it is absolutely the case that the commitment to the ideals of the Constitution by the Justices has been unwavering. Not everyone would have it in his or her heart to shake hands with someone who was involved in their assassination attempt. In accordance with the best side of his idealism, Sachs shook this young man's hand only after he had testified before the TRC. In a sense, then, he insisted that that young man also live up to the ideals of the new dispensation. Sachs's judgments will always be remembered for his unwavering commitment to the ideals for which he risked his life and which he stood by as a judge.

Chapter 2

Abandoning certitudes, becoming human — for a jurisprudence of generosity: an essay in tribute to the work of Albie Sachs[1]

Karin van Marle

> It is about the capacity of abandoning certitudes acquired through a history of habit.
>
> N. S. Ndebele, *Fine Lines from the Box: Further Thoughts about our Country* (Cape Town: Umuzi, 2007), p. 221

Introduction

My aim in this chapter is to give tribute to the enormous contribution made by Albie Sachs to post-apartheid jurisprudence. The project that has occupied most of my research and, to be honest, interest and passion over the past few years is the notion of the becoming of a post-apartheid jurisprudence — the judgments[2] and writings of Albie Sachs play a significant role in such a becoming. Drawing on Drucilla Cornell's engagement with Jacques Derrida, I have previously argued that Sachs's approach to law and jurisprudence hints at the possibility of an alternative understanding of love, *lovance*.[3] In this chapter, I reflect on how to my mind the writings of Sachs disclose and suggest pathways for a post-apartheid jurisprudence. My reflection on a post-apartheid jurisprudence includes an engagement with judgment and specifically judgment in a post-apartheid context. Sachs has offered multiple and a rich variety of angles to jurisprudence and judgment and I elaborate on these below.

Antjie Krog's consideration of the notion of becoming in the book, *Begging to be Black*, has significant implications for how we understand and respond to post-apartheid becoming, being, and a post-apartheid jurisprudence.[4] Krog relies on a Deleuzian notion of becoming, becoming in the sense of becoming minor.[5] For Deleuze, all becoming would mean becoming minor because it requires a shift from the standard or norm. Krog relying on this understanding of becoming is interested in transforming into something new, "in what kind of self I should grow into in order to live a caring, useful and informed life ... within southern Africa."[6]

I read the main concern and question posed by her, and most pertinently articulated by the title of the book, as the question of how to be ethical, how

Albie Sachs reading at the People's Congress

Source: Albie Sachs documentary collection at the Mayibuye Centre.

to respond in an ethical manner to the continuance of injustice in a post-apartheid setting. This question is then also the question that should be central to post-apartheid jurisprudence. I tentatively argue for an angle that might push law to give up exactly what makes it law, its certitude, and thereby expose law to the possibility/experiment of becoming more human. My contention is that the jurisprudence of Albie Sachs, his writings on, and engagements with, law stand in the guise of law giving up, or at least doubting certitude and becoming more human.

One of the concerns, if not the primary concern, facing law and jurisprudence in the aftermath of apartheid is that of transformation: how to ensure that the shifts from parliamentary sovereignty to constitutional supremacy, from totalitarianism, racism, and sexism to democracy, and from authoritarianism to a culture of justification will result in substantive change, beyond a mere change in form. Mahmood Mamdani's response to the Truth and Reconciliation Commission, noting that it might have brought about a limited form of political reconciliation (between what he calls victims in the minority and perpetrators) but failed to achieve social reconciliation (between the majority of victims and beneficiaries), is of importance.[7] His distinction can be connected to Cornell's argument on two types of transformation and notably how transformation should be distinguished from evolution. Transformation in her view entails not only a radical change of a system, but also the change of the subjects within the system.[8] The idea of post-apartheid law becoming human by giving up certitudes could be one attempt to bring about a substantive transformation that goes beyond a mere change in form and that could contribute to the social reconciliation sought by Mamdani. My argument in this chapter is that Sachs's contribution to post-apartheid jurisprudence through his judgments, but also beyond this — his writings and reflections on judgment, has played a significant role in opening paths for such a transformation.

Before I continue, I want to briefly recall the search by Douzinas and Gearey to return to what they call a "general jurisprudence."[9] They lament the shift from general jurisprudence to restricted jurisprudence, a process by which jurisprudence has been preoccupied with the question "What is law?", "an endless interrogation of the essence of substance of law."[10] The result of such a restricted jurisprudence was that the enquiry of jurisprudence, what is considered relevant, is limited to a small number of institutions, practices, and actors, with many excluded. A general jurisprudence encompasses a wider concern, examines a greater number of aspects: it is "concerned not just with posited law, but also with what can be called the law of the law."[11] General jurisprudence has a much wider concept of legality, which includes issues such as social being and social existence: "[G]eneral jurisprudence examines ways in which subjectivity is created as a site of freedom and of subjection."[12] It is my contention that post-apartheid jurisprudence should situate itself within general jurisprudence — the influence of Albie Sachs, his configurations of the alchemy of life and law stand in the guise of a general jurisprudence. Douzinas and Gearey emphasize the double meaning of jurisprudence, which simultaneously refers to law's consciousness — the prudence, wisdom, and phronesis of law (and its conscience), the explorations of law's justice, the ideal law.[13] Post-apartheid jurisprudence, the jurisprudence in the aftermath of an authoritarian and violent past, cannot only be the consciousness of law, but must also involve a deep and continuous exploration of law's conscience.

In my own engagement with post-apartheid jurisprudence, I have reflected on the notions of ethical equality, slowness, memorial constitutionalism, and refusal as possible ways to problematize law's grand narrative and monumental gesture.[14] These notions, by raising the limits of substantive equality, the problems of generalization and the lack of what Simone Weil calls "attention" in law's time, arguing for a constitutionalism embedded in memory, remembering the past and not merely celebrating the present, and refusing the pervasiveness of law, all pushed for law's conscience to come to the fore.

It is against this background that I reflect on the jurisprudence of Albie Sachs. I have previously argued, following Patricia Williams, for a jurisprudence of generosity that possibly captures my view on Sachs's work.[15] What lies at the heart of the notion of generosity for me is the idea of unexpectedness that breaks with the formality and predictability of law — it is this unexpectedness that could disclose new directions of thinking about and doing law.[16] A jurisprudence of generosity, of course, stands in the guise of a general jurisprudence, as discussed above. Sachs's approach could be regarded as one of generosity, in all senses of the word. In the context of law and jurisprudence, generosity indicates for me a willingness to look widely, to stretch and push, to include many angles, to be unpredictable, but also to become human, and encompasses thus in a sense a certain kind of humanism. Below I relate this understanding of generosity with two further notions: firstly, a certain understanding of modernity (Afro-modernism) as put forward by Achille Mbembe and Sarah Nuttal; and, secondly, an Arendtian notion of judgment relying on worldliness and plurality.[17]

Three themes central in the work of Albie Sachs — namely, alchemy, uBuntu, and restorative justice — each in its own way could work towards law's doubting/giving up of certitude and becoming more human — towards a jurisprudence of generosity. The notion of the alchemy of life and law disrupts and problematizes the strict divides between law, politics, morality, ethics, and the social. We should consider if an alternative understanding of space and time comes to the fore through this disruption, thereby disclosing an understanding that is different from traditional Western understanding of space and time.

UBuntu can be regarded as asking for exactly an alternative understanding of time and space, an understanding that urges different questions from the predictable when and where ones. My own support of uBuntu is one that aspires to the potential of taking up uBuntu as an instance of critique, uBuntu as unsettling the certainty of a Western liberal order, as opening the insurgent elements of law.[18]

Concerning restorative justice, one could argue that what might be central in restorative justice is the striving towards law or at least a legal response that could be more human. This response is only possible after the giving up of certainty, the acceptance of finitude. George Pavlich's critical reflection on what he calls the "paradoxes of restorative justice" must be taken into account, namely that it is not an approach that stands in contrast to law, but rather one that strengthens law.[19] Berkowitz and Cornell, reflecting on the Eastwood film, *Mystic River*, illustrate the difference between asserting sovereignty and/or becoming human.[20] My tentative argument is that Sachs's approach to law, jurisprudence, and judgment stands in the guise of law becoming human, attempting to recognize finitude rather than asserting sovereignty.[21] As Berkowitz and Cornell note, this kind of giving up, acceptance of finitude could be "frightening," it could bring discomfort. I argue that the question at the heart of post-apartheid jurisprudence itself, how to be ethical, always already embraces the finitude of law, and what Foucault calls "the ethics of discomfort."[22]

In the writings of Sachs, including his judgments, on the alchemy (and sometimes he says unity) of life and law, uBuntu, and restorative justice, one finds a certain optimism, romanticism — a view of the Constitution as monumental and grand. However, one also finds in the same gesture his realization of finitude, a drive for law to become human that might undermine, disrupt, and shake the optimism and romanticism. In this chapter I want to link the tension (alchemy) between optimism about law's potential (law/the Constitution as monument) and a recognition of law's finitude (law/the Constitution as memorial) with a contemplation on modernity (and a focus on Johannesburg as metropolis and instantiation of modernity). As I discuss below, the exposure of worldliness, cosmopolitanism, humanism, as well as ambiguity and complexity, is of significance for a certain notion of judgment subscribed to by Sachs. My argument is that Sachs's jurisprudence illustrates exactly a rich worldliness and cosmopolitanism and complex humanism. I elaborate on this below.

The chapter unfolds as follows: I start by discussing some of the thoughts and reflections raised by Sachs on judgment and refer briefly to some of his judgments. I then refer to an exchange between Stuart Woolman and Albie Sachs that took place few years ago. My interest is Woolman's description of the South African Constitution as the "last great modernist project," his reasoning for describing the South African Constitution as such, and Sachs's tactful response.[23] From here, I engage with Achille Mbembe and Sarah Nuttal's reflections on what they call African modernity as a way to problematize Woolman's description of modernism. I have previously linked the approach of Mbembe and Nuttal to a critical understanding of transformative constitutionalism, and I extend it here to the jurisprudence and approach to judgment of Albie Sachs.[24] I then turn to a piece by Jonathan Hyslop on Johannesburg as a site of modernity and the role it played in shaping the politics of Mahatma Ghandi and Nelson Mandela.[25] Sachs (albeit from Cape Town and not Johannesburg) displays an embrace of complexity in his approach to law similar to that which Hyslop attributes to the politics of Ghandi and Mandela. After this, I briefly reflect on judgment with reference to the notion developed by Hannah Arendt and commentators on her work. I conclude by placing Albie Sachs's approach to law, jurisprudence, and judgment within the guise of modernity as described by Mbembe, Nuttal, and Hyslop, and bringing it back to the idea of abandoning certitude, becoming human, and a jurisprudence of generosity.

"Now as a judge I found myself puzzled by how difficult it was to be logical"[26]

Albie Sachs in *The Alchemy of Life and Law* reflects on his time on the bench and shares his views on judgment with a wide public. In the book, he elaborates on some of the views that he has mentioned in his response to Stu Woolman briefly referred to below. It is not for me to summarize the arguments that are beautifully and elegantly presented in the book. I will highlight a few remarks made in the chapter on "Reason and judgment."[27] Sachs describes how it was impossible to make a decision being led by either life experience or dogmatic rules. He recalls a conversation with Jennifer Nedelsky in which she summarized Arendt's embrace of Kantian reflective judgment. Inspired by her explanation of reflective judgment, Sachs continues to describe his experience of judgment as not the outcome of logic, but simultaneously not pure personal taste: "It is the outcome of an evaluation, of a weighing . . ."[28] and it is a "public act, with public consequences."[29] He also highlights the importance of realizing that a judgment must be accepted by a community, a judgment must relate to some kind of common understanding. Pure reasoning is one aspect of the process of judging, but only one. It is also noteworthy that he rejects any notion that a decision could have an inevitable outcome. The notion of enlarged mentality adopted by Arendt from Kant is for him one of the elements of control, that a judgment must always consider the standpoint of others. The fact that multiple judges are involved in a judgment is another factor that enables individual preferences and prejudices to counteract each other. He regards the public nature of judgments as another disciplining factor.

Another aspect of his recollection of judgment that for me clearly illustrates the humility with which he approaches judgment is his reference to "a modesty inherent in the judicial function."[30] This feeling of modesty prevented him from believing that any specific judgment is necessarily the right one, but importantly he adds that this has nothing to do with being personally humble: "My modesty is institutional, not personal."[31] Elaborating on his view that the judicial function is not about being right, he says:

> We give it our best shot, knowing that our judgments will enter the list and engage with endless other judgments, many still to be written, in the timeless tournament of competing and converging legal ideals.[32]

This description resonates with Hannah Arendt's reference to Penelope, that the work of the night before can always be undone and yet done again.[33] The idea of judgment as an endless process of weaving and unweaving is suggested here. We must remember that Penelope was banned from her home by her son to the servant quarters. Being homeless, she managed to create a space, a home, amidst uncertainty. Refusing the demands by her suitors, but in a sense also the expectations of her husband Odysseus when she doesn't recognize him at first on his return, she constructs an alternative way of being.[34] In a sense, Sachs in his approach to law, jurisprudence, and judgment can be read as refusing the positivism and formalism of dominant approaches by creating, weaving, and unweaving a web of other possibilities, a law that is generous and becoming human.

A final remark from Sachs's chapter on reason and judgment is the centrality that he gives to the imagination when judging. He tells how when writing a judgment he not only thought of his colleagues on the constitutional court, other judges, and magistrates, but also imagined legal practitioners, ordinary people, members of government, academics, and law students. The active use of the imagination is not only central to reflective or aesthetic judgment, but is true to the understanding of generosity that I attempt to put forward. The process of imagining does not only widen the scope of the judgment, but has a humanizing aspect, underscoring the necessity to make judgments that affect people, the world knowing that the outcome will be uncertain and unstable.

Looking at just a few of Sachs's judgments could illustrate his approach to judgment discussed above. For our purposes here, it is of importance to read these judgments as reflective, as generous, and as worldly. William Smith identifies three features of worldliness, which he draws from Hannah Arendt.[35] Firstly, worldliness is described as "a particular mode of being in the world."[36] It mediates our relations with others, with emphasis on self-reflexivity. It is important that there exists a certain distance between people. Worldliness does not imply "feelings of security, warmth and belonging, or the sensation of being at ease in the world."[37] As Dana Villa puts it: "[T]o be worldly in Arendt's sense is to inscribe a certain modality of alienation at the heart of one's existence and to give this alienation an extremely positive valorization."[38] Smith explains the second feature as closely connected to the first, namely a "heightened care for the world." He interprets this care as having an interest in what goes on in the world, in wanting to talk to others about it, and to be concerned with its durability. This care for the world is associated with a kind of "humanism," explained by Arendt as "the result of the *cultura animi*, of an attitude that knows how to take care and preserve and admire the things of the world."[39] Again, it should be noted that this does not mean having compassion or pity, but rather having a concern with, for example, the creation of a public space, the possibility for action and speech. The third feature connects strongly with the first two, namely "the manner of our disclosures to the world."[40] Political action and speech in the public realm, but, importantly, also judgment are ways of disclosure. According to Fine, "being worldly involves talking with others, seeing things from alternative points of view, formulating an opinion on the matter at hand and seeking to persuade others of the soundness of one's view."[41]

These features are important for a contemplation of the notion of generosity, a jurisprudence of generosity and generous judging that we find in the judgments of Sachs. Generosity indicates worldliness, a way of connecting abstract rules and doctrine with context, not a thoughtless sentimentality lacking rigor. The abandoning of certitude and recognition of finitude and how it relates to becoming human and a new kind of humanism, are central to the becoming of not only a post-apartheid jurisprudence, but also post-apartheid being as such. I refer below to a few of his judgments.

In the case of *Harksen* v. *Lane*,[42] the plaintiff argued that section 21 of the Insolvency Act, which stipulated that the estates of spouses merge in a case of one partner's insolvency, violated amongst others the equality guarantee in section 8 of the interim Constitution. The majority of the Court found that the section does not violate the equality provision. Sachs, in a minority judgment with Kate O'Regan, argued that the section affronts the personal dignity of persons involved in a marital relationship and perpetuates an archaic vision of marriage. He found that the section was patriarchal in origin, promoting a concept of marriage in which, independently of the living circumstances and careers of the spouses, their estates merged. The underlying premise of this section is that "one business mind is at work in marriage, not two."[43] Sachs described this section as reinforcing a stereotypical view of marriage, which, in light of the values of the Constitution, is demeaning to both spouses.

In the case of *Jordan*,[44] Sachs and O'Regan again delivered a minority judgment on the following events. On August 20, 1996, a police officer entered a brothel in Pretoria and paid R250 for a pelvic massage, whereafter arrests were made on the grounds of contravention of the Sexual Offences Act 23 of 1957, which criminalizes providing sex for reward and brothel-keeping. The arrested sex workers argued that certain sections of the Act were unconstitutional, because they amounted to unfair discrimination on sex/gender grounds, because only the acts of sex workers were criminalized, but not the acts of customers. The High Court held that section 20(1)(a) of the Act, which penalized sex for reward, and sections 2, 3(b), and 3(c) of the Act (the brothel provisions), were unconstitutional. The matter was referred to the Constitutional Court for confirmation. The majority of the court rejected the decision taken by the High Court on grounds that the specific sections of the Act were not unconstitutional. Sachs J. and O'Regan J., in a minority judgment, differed and found these sections to be of a discriminatory nature. In their judgment, they noted that "the element of gender is not just happenstance, but integral to the prohibited conduct and constitutive of the way it is treated by the law, enforcement agents and society."[45]

In the *National Coalition*[46] case, the Constitutional Court had to decide on the criminality of sodomy. The decision was that the criminalization of sodomy is unconstitutional, and not true to the values of the Constitution, particularly dignity. Sachs gave a separate judgment in which he concurred with the majority. Significant about his decision is that unlike the decision delivered by Ackerman J., he argued for the respect of sexual choice without reading it through a heteronormative lens. He made the following remark:[47]

> While recognising the unique worth of each person, the Constitution does not presuppose that a holder of rights is as an isolated, lonely and abstract figure possessing a disembodied and socially disconnected self. It acknowledges that people live in their bodies, their communities, their cultures, their places and their times. The expression of sexuality requires a partner, real or imagined. It is not for the state to choose or to arrange the choice of partner, but for the partners to choose themselves.

In *Fourie*,[48] the court had to decide on the constitutionality of the common law definition of marriage that restricted marriage to heterosexual couples. It was decided that this goes against the protection of equality in the Constitution and the legislature was given a year to make legislative amendments. As also noted by De Vos and Barnard-Naude, Sachs's decision here could be seen as simultaneously enabling and disabling — he could have immediately read marriage to mean hetero- and homosexual marriage, but preferred to defer to the legislature.[49] However, with both these cases the Court took the first steps in exposing and questioning the heteronormativity in what was and still is perceived as neutral common law.

In the case of *Volks*,[50] the Court was faced with the question of the inheritance of the estate of a deceased unmarried partner. The majority of the Court decided that the partner cannot inherit. Sachs, in a striking minority judgment, differed from the majority, arguing that formal marriage should not be the yardstick, but whether the couple shared a life together. He answered negatively to the following question posed by himself: "Should marriage be the exclusive touchstone of a survivor's legal entitlement as against the rights of legatees and heirs?" As in *Harksen*, Sachs refuses to follow accepted convention, and instead pauses to think about how the lives of parties are affected by legal formalism.

In the *PE Municipality*[51] case, Sachs raised the possibility that important aspects of an eviction dispute could be resolved through a court order directing the parties to negotiate the solution. He not only recognized the public and political nature of such an action, but displayed a specific care for the world and the relationships embedded in a world. His judgment here is exemplary of the generosity and humanism that underlie his approach to law, jurisprudence, and judging:[52]

> It is not only the dignity of the poor that is assailed when homeless people are driven from pillar to post in a desperate quest for a place where they

> and their families can rest their heads. Our society as a whole is demeaned when state action intensifies rather than mitigates their marginalization.

In the defamation case of *Dikoko*,[53] Mr. Dikoko, the mayor of the Southern District Municipality in the North West Province, aggrieved about being taken to task about his grossly excessive use of a municipal cellphone, said things about Mr. Mokhatla, the municipal manager, that resulted in the latter being awarded an amount of R110,000 on the grounds of defamation. Justice Sachs, in a concurring judgment with Justice Mokgoro, noted the limits of present defamation law in addressing this kind of relation. He argued for developing the common law to make it more consistent with the ethics of the new constitutional order, an ethics that could "facilitate interpersonal repair and the restoration of social harmony."[54] Sachs argued that the common law protection against defamation amounts to treating a person's reputation and honor — inherent features of a person's dignity — as if these were marketplace commodities. He argued as follows:

> Unlike businesses, honor is not quoted on the Stock Exchange. The true and lasting solace for the person wrongly injured is the vindication by the Court of his or her reputation in the community. The greatest prize is to walk away with head high, knowing that even the traducer has acknowledged the injustice of the slur.[55]

As we have seen also in the cases above, his engagement here with these events illustrates his attempt not to assert a sovereign decision making use of the rules of the common law that prescribe a remedy of monetary compensation. Stating that "unlike businesses, honor is not quoted on the Stock Exchange," he pushes for a development of the common law along the lines of uBuntu that could bring about a new kind of ethics. This decision shows the possible promise in law and legal judgment to bring about a new vocabulary, and to play a role in the becoming human of law and society in the aftermath of apartheid.

The examples above show how Sachs has responded to problems brought to the Court in a thoughtful manner. Taking risks, he never shied away from being unpredictable, from following new routes. He acted not in a sympathetic or emotional way, but in a manner that illustrated his care for the world, and for the relations between human beings in a world. In deciding (with O'Regan) on equality and discrimination in the case of two married persons in *Harksen*, he was not prepared to follow the patriarchal view that subordinates the female partner (the wife) to the male (the husband). In the sex worker case, he (with O'Regan) dared to name the discrimination on the grounds of sex/gender, thereby challenging the legal claim to a neutral law. In *National Coalition* and *Fourie*, heteronormativity was challenged and in *Fraser* and *Volks*, care was regarded higher than legal exclusion. In *PE Municipality* and *Dikoko*, Sachs considered alternative ways in which to address conflict in the lives of members of a post-apartheid society. I refer to one more decision below that illustrates his belief that there is no correct answer that can be found and stated once and for all.

In *Minister of Health* v. *New Clicks*,[56] a case that dealt with the validity of regulations setting medicine prices, Sachs exhibited a nuanced approached to what by the other judges of the Court was depicted as the either/or question whether or not ministerial regulations are administrative action so that administrative law procedural fairness requirements would apply to their enactment. Whereas a number of the judges on the Court held that such regulations were in a blanket fashion administrative action, Sachs held that regulations could be administrative action, depending on the circumstances in each case. In particular, he pointed out that the nature of the impact of such regulations were determinative: should the regulations, as legislation, have only general impact, they would not be administrative action; but should they have a specific impact in addition, i.e. by affecting a particular person or group of people in a specific manner, apart from their general impact, they would be administrative action, subject to procedural fairness. Here, we see Sachs affirming the importance of judging in context, and in a contextual manner, the importance of caring for the world.

Patricia Williams, in the first few pages of her book, *The Alchemy of Race and Rights*,[57]disgruntled with legal writing that presumes a "legal methodology that is highly stylized, precedential, and based on deductive reasoning," aims to depart from it by creating a genre of legal writing that could fill the gaps of traditional scholarship. She explains that for her these gaps had to be filled in with "connections, connections between psyches, between lived experience and social perception, and between an encompassing historicity and a jurisprudence of generosity."[58] I have previously combined this notion of generosity with the act of refusal as portrayed by, for example: Giorgio Agamben in his description of Herman Melville's Bartleby; the act of refusal by Maurice Blanchot in the context of the French invasion of Algiers; and Adriana Cavarero's re-interpretation of the act of Penelope as refusal.[59] Cavarero is of course an interpreter of Arendt, so it comes as no surprise that Arendt explicitly refers to Penelope's act of weaving in *The Life of the Mind* as referred to by Kant. Explaining that it is impossible to approve of a rule once and for all as if it no longer can be questioned once established as a rule, she writes: "From which it follows that the business of thinking is like Penelope's web; it undoes every morning what it has finished the night before."[60] I have started tentatively to configure a jurisprudence of generosity, and with even greater caution generous judgment, as a way of approaching the law that refuses preconceived, predetermined, predictable, and thoughtless outcomes. Such an approach weaves and unweaves and in refusing the power of certitude and the assertion of sovereignty, finds its own rhythm, time, and space. Within this rhythm, time and space law could confront its finitude and could become human. As Arendt reminds us in her understanding of judgment, this does not mean to have empathy, but to be open to other perspectives, to human plurality, to the world. My argument in this chapter is that the judgments of Albie Sachs could be regarded as generous judgment, his writing and reflections on judgment as a jurisprudence of generosity. In the next section, I turn to Woolman's idea of the South African Constitution as "the last great modernist project" and Sachs's response.

"South Africa remains the last modernist project"[61]

In a chapter entitled "The South African Constitution as the last modernist project," Stu Woolman enters into a conversation with Albie Sachs in response to a remark made by Sachs on the role of legal academics in a post-apartheid South Africa.[62] Woolman, understanding Sachs's remark as implying that legal academics, although they played a role during the transition, will play a lesser role now, reflects on how he (Woolman) conceives of the role of an academic.

Answering his own question on the phenomenological role of academics and what we do, he says, "Well, we fix things."[63] He continues describing his job as an academic as similar to a "mechanic," "therapist," "architect," "mason," and "critic."[64] Therapists, architects, and critics who stand in a different philosophical/theoretical tradition from Woolman might dispute the understanding of their work as being mainly concerned with "fixing," offering solutions and making sense. But then, for Woolman, "such philosophical fashion has not yet taken root here."[65] Therefore, South Africa "remains . . . the last great modernist project."[66] Academics should strive to "get things right. To get as close to the truth as possible."[67]

Part and parcel of this task is to "treat its [the law's] texts with respect." Such respect entails that "we never for a moment deny the law its autonomy," which entails "the recognition that legal texts possess a logic and power of their own."[68] From his description of the South African Constitution as the "last great modernist project," one may summarize the following features of modernity that he ascribes to the (and prescribes for any) constitutional endeavor.

Firstly, "truth," and as Woolman indicates he means truth "with a capital T."[69] Secondly, "rational political discourse," meaning that law should not simply get it right by producing right answers, but also by "getting there the right way," following a sound method. Thirdly, he highlights the commitment to great ideals and the possibility of material transformation through law, or to be more specific through the Constitution. Woolman refers to voices that challenge the potential of law to achieve all of this, but argues that this does not lessen the commitment to the "Enlightenment's commitment to truth."[70] He states that such "philosophical fashion has not taken root here. South Africa remains the last great modernist project."[71]

Below, I turn to a discussion by Achille Mbembe and Sarah Nuttal on the idea of Johannesburg as metropolis, as the symbol of the African modern, which they describe as "a specific way of being in the world."[72] Their take on modernity offers a different view from the one followed by Woolman in his reconfiguring of the South African Constitution as a modernist project. I also engage with a piece by Jonathan Hyslop on "Ghandi, Mandela and the African modern." In both of these pieces, another perspective on modernity is raised that I find significant for an engagement with the South African Constitution as modernist in a specific way and for the crucial role of Albie Sachs in this configuration. But, first, a brief look at Sachs's response to Stu Woolman, because in this response we see traces of Sachs's approach to law, jurisprudence, and judgment.

Sachs starts by indeed referring to the influence that academics had on the first constitutional steps taken by judges: "There was a heady and inspiring spurge of legal energy in academe."[73] Judges, on the other hand, "seemed to be frozen in positivistic time."[74] He poses two questions: the first one concerns the relationship between judges and academics; and the second one the materials that could be used to direct judges in interpreting the Constitution. More pertinently, his first question raises the dominant legal tradition that subscribed to a problematic hierarchical relation between academics and judges. With reference to Max Weber's account of legal scholarship in England, Sachs explains as a possible reason the extent to which the legal profession controls legal education in contrast to Europe.[75] Sachs mentions that the legal profession did not only control the qualifications for legal practice, but got universities to subscribe to the virtues of the profession. He also refers to an address by US Supreme Court Justice Brennan in which he named two important checks on judicial discretion that arose in response to the close links between judges and partisan politics, namely precedent and a public and reasoned explanation of the outcome. Both of these practices had the effect of "distancing" a judge from the outcome of a case and created the appearance that precedent alone determined the result.[76]

With respect to the second question on materials, Sachs reflects on his approach to judgment and states that when writing judgments he was not seeking "authoritative pronouncement," but rather "philosophy, a phrase, a persuasive argument."[77] Sachs's response here to Woolman is interesting: he is not directly opposing him, but his description of the task of a judge, or at least his approach to judgment, and therefore to law and jurisprudence is not the search for truth, correct answers, finding solutions, but a much more tentative, reflective engagement with legal problems as social problems of great complexity. For Sachs, "what we required . . . was prescience rather than precedent."[78] The views by Sachs on judgment stand in contrast to formalist/positivist ways of legal reasoning. His approach is generous, aware of law's as well as a court's finitude, reflecting a kind of humanism in law.

Below, I turn to the notion of the African modern, with the view to situate the approach of Sachs within this framework.

"The African modern is a specific way of being in the world."[79]

Achille Mbembe and Sarah Nuttal describe Johannesburg as "the symbol par excellence of the 'African modern'."[80] As already noted above, they define the African modern as "a specific way of being in the world."[81] They underscore the specific way in which "worldliness" comes to the fore as not only an engagement with domestic cultural forms, institutions, and ways of life, but also with those from elsewhere. For them, modernity and worldliness in the context of Johannesburg have been "intrinsically connected to various forms of circulation — of people, capital, finance, and images — and to overlapping spaces and times."[82] In their work on Johannesburg, they address the way in which the global city has been approached by the dominant paradigm and argue that quite often a purely functionalist theory has been followed, neglecting the complexity of the city. They observe that "a true global city ... is composed not only of flows of money, skills, knowledge . . . but also of ideas, people, images and imaginaries — a cultural economy."[83] I have previously used their argument to view the notion of "transformative constitutionalism" suggested by Karl Klare more than a decade ago and particularly the ways in which South African legal scholars engaged with the notion.[84] My sense was that often the problems that we face as legal scholars are approached in a way that neglects to pay sufficient attention to the complexity of these issues, what the authors phrase as the "cultural economy."[85] For me, the notion of transformative constitutionalism asks for a multiple approach to law, one that does not necessarily subscribe to law's autonomy, if this means the treatment of law and legal texts, also the Constitution, as if they have a life of their own. The reason for returning to this vision of the global city as a complex entity of overlapping aims, functions, ideals, and desire while reflecting on the work of Albie Sachs is because to my mind he gets it — instinctively his approach to law, jurisprudence, and judgment is one that is always true to the law, but one that simultaneously realizes the complexity, the overlapping of many things. Again, an example from administrative law is apposite. In *Sidumo* v. *Rustenburg Platinum Mines*,[86] the central issue was whether a decision taken on arbitration with respect to a labor dispute by the Commission for Conciliation, Mediation and Arbitration amounted to administrative action subject to review in terms of administrative justice rights through the Promotion of Administrative Justice Act 3 of 2000 (the PAJA), or whether it amounted to labour-related judicial conduct subject to review only in terms of section 145 of the Labor Relations Act 66 of 1995 (the LRA). The majority of the Court through Navsa A. J. held that the conduct was administrative action, but nevertheless stood to be reviewed in terms of the LRA, albeit read in light of the PAJA — holding, in other words, that the administrative law applied to the arbitral decision, but through the enforcement institutions of the labor law. Sachs signs on to this outcome, but explains the conclusion in an instructive manner. He points to the futility of compartmentalizing different sets of public law regulation depending on a compartmentalization of different kinds of public conduct. Instead, he argues that all forms of public conduct are hybrid in nature and permit the application of different sets of regulation at the same time. He proposes the development of a "hybrid regulatory system"[87] that would apply to all forms of public conduct, but for which the nature, extent, and strictness of control would depend on the circumstances of each specific case. In short, for him the nature and degree of rules that would apply to any one public decision would "depend more on the nature of the interest at stake in each specific case than the label or labels to be attached"[88] and that judges should "eschew . . . formal pigeonholing" in favor of "integrated reasoning."[89] The focus is clearly, therefore, on the complexity, permeability, and integration of different things.

Mbembe and Nuttal, following the work of James Ferguson, note how most studies on African cities have relied on "an underlying meta-narrative of modernization," urbanization, and crisis.[90] However, what has been neglected is the capacity of African cities also to attract certain forms of initially colonial and now global capital. Globalization for them stands in the guise of exactly these paradoxes of "connection" and "disconnection and exclusion" following processes that are "refracted, splintered and cracked."[91] They are interested in ways of reading the African city that move away from the traditional paradigms, suggesting alternative readings. It is exactly these alternative readings that could illustrate also an alternative for traditional jurisprudence. They refer to works by four authors, namely Jane Guyer, AbdouMaliq Simone, Filip de Boeck, and Rem Koolhaas. Firstly, Guyer highlights the growth of cities along new pathways, incorporating, for example, practices of everyday life in the growth of cities. Instability, specifically monetary instability, and acute shortages are dominant; however, new possibilities emerge. Secondly, they refer to Simone, who focuses on themes of informality, invisibility, spectrality, and movement.[92] The third approach they identify is by de Boeck, who is interested in how the city constantly reconfigures its public and private spaces: "The city in a way, exists beyond its architecture."[93] Fourthly, Koolhaas challenges the opposition between the "formal" and the "unformed" and constructs a third term, namely that of the informal, which he defines as "neither formed nor unformed; alternately it looks like both."[94]

I find all four approaches referred to above suggestive as ways of reflecting on post-apartheid law and jurisprudence. One could argue that Sachs in his engagement with the problems with which legal scholars and the Constitutional Court are faced, recognizing the practices of everyday life, disclosed unknown pathways; noticed and created new possibilities for law, including issues concerning informality, spectrality, the reconfiguring of public and private spaces, and the play between formal and the unformed. Sachs's separate opinion in *New Clicks* again provides an example of this. He formulates, or "forms" a rule — regulations can be administrative action depending on the circumstances of each case and in particular the nature of the impact of those regulations. But it is a rule that is formed anew every time it is applied — the facts of each case determine each and every time whether or not a regulation is administrative action.

Mbembe and Nuttal seek to read the city as more than "simply a string of infrastructures, technologies, and legal entities": they want to expose that it also consists of "actual bodies, images, forms, footprints, and memories."[95] Their aim is to highlight the "artistic and aesthetic" elements of the city. "Rather than opposing the 'formal' and the 'informal', or the 'visible' and the 'invisible,'" they call for a "more complex anthropology of things, forms, signs."[96] As noted above, it is such an approach that in my view should be translated to and expanded to post-apartheid jurisprudence, one that Sachs initiated in his writings. Such an approach also gives another angle to the argument of law's autonomy, without directly opposing it; it problematizes, refractures the claim. For example, by acknowledging how the "'informal' itself expresses a 'form,'" hiding and revealing rationalities, the multiplicity of law in all forms could come to the fore. The authors observe that many descriptions of Africa aim to describe it as "otherworldly," "apart from the world," a "failed or incomplete example of something else."[97] Their aim is to problematize the sameness/difference dichotomy, making space for "the originality of the African modern, its capacity to produce something new and singular" to become visible. Post-apartheid law, perhaps particularly in the development of a jurisprudence that takes uBuntu seriously, has already produced original and new angles. Sachs has been central to this.

Mbembe and Nuttal observe that in many writings "modernity has been perceived as nothing more than the development of the capitalist mode of production and the processes by which capitalism as a socioeconomic formation in turn transformed social relations and the consciousness of black urban dwellers."[98] Charles van Onselen, for example, describes Johannesburg as a city caught up in self-interest, struggle, shallowness, "generations [that] have always felt more comfortable in the bank, the stock exchange and the sports stadium than they have in attending a church, sitting in a concert hall, walking through an art gallery, reading in a library or even serving in the ranks of their city council."[99] With some tweaking, these words could fit with how many people (legal scholars included) perceive law and legal practice and sadly legal scholarship. A jurisprudence of generosity could problematize such a one-dimensional vision of and for law and unlock its potential, as was seen in the jurisprudence of Sachs, for example, in the cases of *Dikoko* and *PE Municipality* discussed above.

Mbembe and Nuttal search to bring in also other perspectives on Johannesburg, exposing how the "city always operates as a site of fantasy, desire, and imagination."[100] They describe how South African historiography tends to approach the city in a way that neglects to go beyond a certain point. They distinguish broadly between three approaches. Firstly, a line that is concerned with spatial dislocation, class differentiation, and racial polarization focusing, for example, on poverty and forced removals. These studies aptly describe racial forms of dispossession and exclusion. Mbembe and Nuttal note how these versions perceive the city merely as "a space of planning" and not as an "aesthetic project."[101] A second line focuses on institutional governance, deracialization of service provision, and local politics, but fails to acknowledge that which goes beyond these, "city-ness as such." For this approach, the city is a problem that must be solved, and in this vein *they* prescribe what is to be done.[102] A third line focuses on the spatial restructuring of the city, noting the construction of offices, complexes, upper class residences. The authors critique these studies and highlight two aspects: firstly, the necessity to formulate theories of race, class, labor, and capital that are more sensitive to the underlying complexities, particularly the violent past of apartheid; and, secondly, the failure of these theories to engage with the "city-ness" of Johannesburg that could include a vast array of new perspectives. I have previously contemplated to what extent these three features could be true also of approaches to law, specifically approaches to transformative constitutionalism, placing all the emphasis on problem solving, planning, restructuring in such a way as to render more complex theories and engagements with ideas and the imagination worthless.[103] Sachs, in his carefully considered judgments, displayed an awareness of the complexities of the legal problems dealt with by judges, and the necessity of a plurality of perspectives as a response.

Mbembe and Nuttal refer to works that explore modernity in places like China or Brazil, employing an angle that allows "multiple modernities" and the "diversity of universals."[104] In the writings of, for example, Georg Simmel, Walter Benjamin, and Max Weber, metropolitan life encompasses "processes of abstraction, circulation, movement, representation," but importantly also "the responses of the emotions and the mind to these processes."[105] Metropolitan or city life is not so much about the construction of the city as about how it is lived — "exhibited, displayed, and represented, its colorfulness, its aura and its aesthetics."[106] Albie Sachs, in his approach to law and jurisprudence, displayed more of an interest and concern with the lives of people affected by law and the aesthetics of the legal endeavor and less with the abstraction of law. An example of interest and concern is to be found in his judgment in the case of *S* v. *M*.[107] The case dealt with the question of whether the lower courts, in sentencing a primary care-giver of young children convicted of a criminal offence to a term of imprisonment, had paid sufficient regard to the best interests of the children as required by section 28(2) constitutional imprimatur that in all matters concerning children their best interests should be paramount. Sachs responds in his judgment to an argument that this requirement, applying potentially as it does to any case involving children, however indirectly, and prescribing nothing to determine what a child's best interests entail, is too flexible and vague to be useful as a legal standard, as follows:

> ... [I]t is precisely the contextual nature and the inherent flexibility of section 28 that constitutes the source of its strength. . . . [I]ndeterminacy of outcome is not a weakness. A truly principled child-centered approach requires a close and individualized examination of the precise real-life situation of the particular child involved. To apply a predetermined formula for the sake of certainty, irrespective of the circumstances, would in fact be contrary to the best interests of the child concerned.[108]

Apt for any engagement with law — also post-apartheid law — is not only the visible form, but also what lies beneath. Mbembe and Nuttal observe the importance of acknowledging the necropolis and its influence on the metropolis. As stated above, also the necropolis/underground should not be perceived as a mere abstract space in technical terms, but as a space of sociality that inhabits social relations. It is also a space "of suffering and alienation as well as of rebellion and insurrection."[109] This perception of the "underneath," the "concealed or embedded other orders of visibility," is often neglected in legal studies, and in the interpretation of legal texts. Post-apartheid jurisprudence should be cautious not to neglect these "scripts that are not reducible to the built form, the house facade, or simply the street experience of the metaphorical figure of the flaneur."[110]

The essays in the volume are concerned with African modernity, attempting to expand and debunk dominant meanings of the African modern. One aspect is to attempt to expose the gap between the way in which things appear and the way things are. The title of the volume, describing Johannesburg as the elusive metropolis, refers to the impossibility of capturing the city and all its elements, life forms, and heart beats. Mbembe and Nuttal attribute to Johannesburg a "quite unprecedented African cosmopolitanism: the Afropolitan." For them, "it is an original city, speaking in an original voice. Even in its most self-destructive moments, it is a place where a new and singular metropolitan vocabulary is being born."[111] Conceding that the metaphor of a city can have only limited comparison to the notion of law, jurisprudence, and constitutionalism, I am nevertheless intrigued by the possibilities, the suggestion that a post-apartheid jurisprudence can at least contribute to such metropolitan vocabulary — the first steps already taken by, as indicated above, Albie Sachs. Below, I turn to Jonathan Hyslop, who in the volume on Johannesburg reflects on "Ghandi, Mandela and the African modern."[112]

"The modernist energies of his metropolis would prove irrepressible"[113]

Hyslop starts his piece by recalling a bookshop known as Vanguard Booksellers, owned by Russian immigrant, Fanny Klennerman. Klennerman, according to Hyslop, perceived herself as part of a cultural avant-garde and part of a certain modernist movement. Klennerman, Hyslop tells us, was the first person to import Joyce's *Ulysses* to South Africa, a book exemplary of a certain modernism that at the time was banned in the English world. Hyslop is interested in how Johannesburg is part of the story of modernity and modernist culture. He discusses the politics of Johannesburg and its influence on Ghandi and Mandela against the background of Joyce's *Ulysses*. It is important to note the definitions of modern and modernist that guide his investigation. He quotes Marshal Berman:

> To be modern . . . is to experience personal and social life as a maelstrom to find one's world and oneself in perpetual disintegration and renewal, trouble and anguish, ambiguity and contradiction: to be part of a universe in which all that is solid melts into air. To be a modernist is to make oneself somehow at home in the maelstrom, to make its rhythms one's own, to move within its currents in search of reality, of beauty, of freedom, of justice, that its fervid and perilous flow allows.[114]

He describes Johannesburg as instantiation of a form of modernity, as a place of simultaneously "uncertainty and disintegration" and a place that allowed the "search for the possibilities of freedom," "a city of ideas."[115] An important element of the city that he highlights is the capability to go "beyond its immediate confines."[116] It is exactly the possibility and/or impossibility of the law to extend its immediate confines that is of interest to me and crucial to the becoming of a post-apartheid jurisprudence, and what I see in the jurisprudence of Sachs. He observes certain features of the Johannesburg of the early 1930s. With a population of half a million and immigrants coming from all over the world, it hosted a plurality of people and perspectives. The buildings in the city, for example, exhibited a range of different styles from Victorian to Edwardian to Chicago steel frame construction. There were also extreme social inequalities among the inhabitants that often gave rise to conflict and uncertainty. However, for Hyslop, "this very extremity . . . made its experience of modernity productive of modernist cultural and political creativity."[117] The absence of stability, living in the maelstrom, made it possible for people to make themselves at home, for finding new paths. The fact that individuals were uprooted produced new forms of intellectuality and generated new ideas.[118] South Africa of the early 1990s and of course the first term of the Constitutional Court on which Albie Sachs served experienced exactly this kind of newness that could have generated new ideas.

It is in this vein that Hyslop places Fanny Kellerman within the frame of modernity, pursuing a modernist project. And it is exactly within the context of such a modernist project that he situates the development of the political thought of Ghandi and Mandela. I am interested in how these descriptions of modernity and the pursuance of a modernist project relate to Stu Woolman's description of the South African Constitution as modernist project. It seems as if the insistence on solving problems, finding truth asserted by Woolman, is somewhat apart from the descriptions of instability, the maelstrom that we find here. For my purposes here, of course, Sachs's position and engagement with modernity is on the cards.

Hyslop notes that to situate Ghandi and Mandela within the Afro-modern offered by Johannesburg highlights the problem of the tension between the metropolis and nationalism. He mentions that both Ghandi and Mandela, although they started out from narrow nationalism, famously managed to transcend this to approaches that were inclusive, embraced humanistic values, and had international relevance.[119] Hyslop's argument is that their approaches of inclusive nationalism founded on universalist values can be traced to their experience with the metropolitanism and cosmopolitanism of Johannesburg.

Joyce's interrogation of nationalism in *Ulysses* stands in the background of Hyslop's reflections on Ghandi and Mandela. Joyce draws on the Odysseus myth where the Cyclops, the one-eyed giant, captures Odysseus and his crew in his cave and starts to eat them two by two. Only after killing the giant do they manage to escape. In Joyce, the "extreme nationalist" plays the role of the one-eyed giant seeing only from his viewpoint of fanaticism. The character Bloom stands in contrast to this single viewpoint by looking with a two-eyed cosmopolitan empathy. Hyslop notes that Joyce does not dismiss all aspects of nationalism, but realizes the importance of balance, of relativizing nationalism. Bloom acknowledges the ambiguity and complexity of the world.[120] He observes that although modern nationalism has its roots in the metropolis and its according cosmopolitanism, national identity often denies these origins. Referring to a famous passage in another novel by Joyce,[121] where Stephan Daedalus is talking to the headmaster, Mr. Deasey, about the official history told by state and church and refers to a shout in the street as God, Hyslop, following Berman, argues that this character is saying that God (history) is not in the "repressive myths of nation and religion," but in the ambiguous embrace of what is modern as expressed in the everyday of the street.[122] Hyslop's concern is to highlight the tension between nationalism and relativism in political forms rooted in modernity. I want to consider, very tentatively, a link between a certain form of political nationalism and this kind of nationalism in law, for argument's sake subscribing to law's autonomy. But before that, a few references to Hyslop's placing of Ghandi and Mandela and their politics within the metropolis of Johannesburg.

Hyslop recalls Mohandas Ghandi addressing a mass meeting in Johannesburg in 1908 and describes this as the beginning of "a notion of Indian identity that cut through the barriers of religion, class, caste and language."[123] For him, Ghandi was able to create this line of politics rooted in nationalism but subscribing to humanistic universalism that was open to diversity because of being situated in Johannesburg. Johannesburg as the symbol of the African modern exhibiting uncertainty, rupture, and inhabited with people from all over the world, and therefore also enriched by a wide range of intellectualisms, provided a unique context for the development of a new Indian nationalism. Mandela had a similar path. Starting out as a dedicated follower of Anton Lembede's firm African nationalism, he ended up putting forward a vision for a unified and reconciled country that included a plurality of perspectives.[124] As with Ghandi, Hyslop argues that it was Mandela's "metropolitan experience" that nurtured his striving for personal freedom of the metropolis.

Hyslop ends the chapter on a tragic note, reflecting on the extent to which both Ghandi's and Mandela's projects had to succumb to the one-eyed Cyclops of nationalism. The humanist embrace of Ghandi and Nehru was replaced by the sectarianism of Advani and Vajpayee. In the case of Mandela, Hyslop notes the rise of "ethnicism."[125] The end takes a slight upturn when he refers to South African author Charles Bosman's (a "quintessentially Johannesburg character") description of a rupture of a meeting led by Nationalist Party leader D. F. Malan in 1945. Bosman writes: "I breathed a sigh of relief. It was only the spirit of Johannesburg once more asserting itself."[126] Hyslop takes comfort in this, relieved for his part by Bosman's understanding of the irrepressible modernist energies of the metropolis of Johannesburg.

I began this chapter by mentioning my interest in the becoming of a post-apartheid jurisprudence and that central to such a jurisprudence is the giving up of certitudes, the embrace of uncertainty, accepting the finitude of the law instead of re-asserting the power of law and rights that affirm the status quo. In my view, the writings of and approach of Albie Sachs disclose the beginnings of such an approach. This does not mean that Sachs is in any sense disloyal to or disrespectful of the law — one could argue that this stance of his is even because of his loyalty to and respect for the law. Sachs is acutely aware of not only the form of law, the abstract "textbook phrases," but how law affects lives. I described his approach as one of generosity that amounts to the ability to look widely and include multiple perspectives. Inescapably, part of this generosity is a certain humanism, the ability to look beyond narrow concerns of the parochial. I then turned to a description by a South African legal scholar of the South African Constitution as the last modernist project. Woolman, in this description, seemingly associates such a project with the search for truth, with problem solving, with providing answers, and with the belief in law's potential to bring about change. He claims that the philosophical tradition disputing these claims has not taken root in South Africa. My aim is not to take issue with the latter claim, but rather to suggest other takes on modernity as described by the engagements with Johannesburg as symbol of the African modern. An important issue for Woolman is that of law's autonomy — that one should acknowledge the autonomy of the texts of the law. By drawing on Hyslop and his engagement with Joyce's critique on nationalism, I want to raise a concern about law's nationalism, the extent to which the engagement of legal scholars with the law treats it with a one-eyed vision neglecting to see the complexity and ambiguity. Sachs par excellence managed to avoid the vision of the Cyclops approaching the law with an angle of the cosmopolitan, allowing otherworldly influences to seep into law. The Cyclops always hits back, but then the spirit of the city also continues to assert itself. Below, I tentatively reflect on the notion of judgment as it comes to the fore in the thought of Hannah Arendt, who famously rejected all forms of rigid nationalism and identity politics and for whom the love of the world, worldliness, stood central to political thought as well as judgment. For the purpose of this chapter, I want to connect Arendt's notion of judgment that stands in the guise of plurality, cosmopolitanism, and worldliness with the notion of the Afro-modern and the reflections on Johannesburg as metropolis and ultimately with the jurisprudence of Albie Sachs.

Judgment, worldliness, understanding

As stated previously, I am interested in the connections between an Arendtian notion of judgment and the descriptions of modernity, the metropolis, and cosmopolitanism described above in reflections on Johannesburg. One could also draw lines between Albie Sachs's approach to judgment and the notion of judgment supported by Arendt. Immediate lines are those of worldliness and cosmopolitanism, but also the rejection of pure functionalism, thoughtlessness, and importantly the rejection of predictability and the kind of nationalism associated with the Cyclops discussed above.

Seyla Benhabib describes Hannah Arendt as a "reluctant modernist" moving away from interpretations that situate her firmly as anti-modern, as exhibiting a nostalgic longing for a revival of the Greek polis.[127] Many commentators disagree: for Dana Villa, for example, Arendt "barely qualifies as even a reluctant modernist."[128] He follows Kateb's reading of her as a "great antimodernist."[129] My aim here is not to comment on the validity of these conflicting interpretations. I want to put forward briefly what Benhabib calls "a different genealogy of modernity" in Arendt's writings on the "rise of the social."[130]

She finds three dominant meanings of the term "social" in Arendt, namely: the reference to the growth of a capitalist commodity exchange economy; the reference to the rise and growth of mass society; and lastly the reference to sociability. It is sociability that is of relevance for our purposes here. Benhabib notes how Arendt exposes the ongoing tension between "equality" and "difference" in the social and political realms as a feature of modernity.[131] Difference and otherness in pre-modern societies were less prominent because of the exclusion of those who did not fall within the ambits of the homogenized city state. The rise of modernity and Enlightenment promises of political and legal equality made difference real. Benhabib refers here to Arendt's work on anti-Semitism and how it brought the dialectic of equality and difference to the fore. Significant is her description of the "complicated and multilayered ... dynamics of the social."[132] According to Benhabib, when Arendt refers to the social she means sociability: "patterns of human interaction; modalities of taste in dress, eating, leisure, and lifestyles generally; differences in aesthetic, religious, and civic manners and outlooks; patterns of socializing and forming marriages, friendships, acquaintanceships, and commercial exchanges."[133] The social designates "civil and associational society, that sphere of human relations that is not economic, or political, or military, or bureaucratic-administrative."[134]

For Benhabib, in Arendt's biography on Rahel Varnhagen, who ran a Berlin salon in the early nineteenth century, this notion of the social and sociability is at stake. Varnhagen's salon was "a space of sociability in which the individual desire for difference and distinctiveness could assume an intersubjective reality."[135] This notion of sociability also informs her reflections on judgment later in her life. For Benhabib, Arendt's biography of Rahel Varnhagen hints at different interpretations of her understanding of modernity. In what Benhabib calls "an alternative genealogy," modernity is regarded as more than the rise of commodity exchange relations and capitalism and the rise of mass society — it is associated with bringing forth new forms of social relations, of being in the world.[136] This take on modernity connects with the depictions of modernity, Johannesburg as metropolis, and the Afro-modern discussed above. My argument concerning Sachs is that his jurisprudence and judgments confronted and struggled with exactly plural forms of social relations and social being in post-apartheid South Africa.

The concepts of the world, worldliness, and worldlessness play an important role throughout the writings of Arendt. She was interested in specifically the modern condition of "homelessness."[137] Arendt in this vein was influenced by *existenz* philosophy in the work of amongst others Kierkegaard, Nietzsche, Jaspers, Sartre, and Heidegger, naming the loss of human reason, but also the loss of a shared world.[138] Benhabib argues that Arendt brought forward a significant shift in Heidegger's concept of the world by making being in the world, and being with others, central to how worldliness is experienced. Her notion of human plurality that is central to her political and philosophical writings is, according to Benhabib, a forceful response to *existenz* philosophy, most notably the work of Heidegger.[139]

Of relevance for an Arendtian notion of judgment is not only the substantive content of what Benhabib calls her "alternative genealogy/archeology of modernity," but also the methodological angle.[140] Benhabib mentions her use of fragmentary historiography inspired by Walter Benjamin as "an attempt to think through the human history sedimented in layers of language and concepts."[141] In identifying moments of "rupture, displacement and dislocation in history," language plays a significant role. At stake is "a remembering, in the sense of a creative act of rethinking that sets free the lost potentials of the past."[142]

Arendt also shared the views of her life partner, Heinrich Blucher, for whom judgment was not about the following of rules, but rather about examples presented in the imagination.[143] Arendt regarded judgment as always exercised in relationship with others: "visiting others — physically or in your mind — consulting them, seeing things from their point of view, exchanging opinions with them, persuading them, wooing their consent."[144] Following Kant, judgment for her meant the reflection of the plurality of possible opinions. She subscribed to a notion of common sense, which meant that experience where an enlarged mentality allows a person to get beyond (transcend) her own subjectivity and reach what could be regarded as a common understanding, common sense.[145] This notion of common sense in contrast to how it is often understood is not something unreflective or instinctive, but the outcome of a transcendental thought process.

As noted by Young Bruehl, judgment for Arendt was the way through which a person became a "world citizen." The exposure to and experience of plurality assist us in seeing the world also from another's perspective, and the more positions that can be made present or taken into account, the more representative judgment will be.[146] This way of judgment that is possible only through imagination is neither objective nor subjective, but rather intersubjective and representative, and is seeking for a relation between particularity and generality. The notion of aesthetic judgment is therefore never about following or applying general rules, but rather an experiment in the imagination.[147] This understanding of reflective judgment is a prerequisite to living in a shared or common world and for the ability to live well. Benhabib also emphasizes the importance of worldliness for Arendt's notion of judgment, which she describes as "an interest in the world and in the human beings who constitute the world, and a firm grasp of where one's own boundaries lie and where those of others begin."[148] She observes how Arendt, by subscribing to the notion of enlarged thought, returns to the theme of "perspectivality of the public word" that originated in her biography on Rahel Varnhagen.[149]

Conclusion

In the pages above, I have made some reflections on the contribution of Albie Sachs to the becoming of a post-apartheid jurisprudence and to a possible approach to post-apartheid judgment. I referred to Antjie Krog's reliance on the Deleuzian notion of becoming minor and tentatively argued that the question of and search for how to be ethical, or respond in an ethical manner to present events, should lie at the heart of a post-apartheid jurisprudence. I related the becoming of a post-apartheid jurisprudence to generosity, abandoning certitude, and recognizing finitude. This could disclose ways for a new kind of humanism. Situating the judgments of Sachs and also a post-apartheid jurisprudence within a broader discussion of modernity and Johannesburg as metropolis is important so that it could be regarded as part of a broader engagement with law, jurisprudence, and judgment. South Africa, our engagement with law, the Constitution, jurisprudence, and judgment should be regarded as part of a larger world. To become post-apartheid in that sense goes beyond the experience of South Africa in response to its past and present, but forms part of a broader engagement with the world. The extent to which someone like Albie Sachs is honored by the world is proof of the wide reach of his work. The South African Constitution could be regarded as reflective of modernity, meaning a way of being modern that engages with the continued disintegration and renewal, and finding "home" in the midst of these uncertainties. To be true to this understanding of the Constitution as modern, the engagements with all legal scholars, from academics to judges, should allow multiple angles, be open to a plurality of views and methods. Responding to the various issues by refusing the assertion of sovereignty and the abandonment of certitude could be part of the search for what Mbembe and Nuttal call a new vocabulary.[150] Sachs's engagements with uBuntu, restorative justice, and writing on the alchemy of life and law have their roots in such a new vocabulary. Drucilla Cornell in this volume in connection to Albie Sachs raises the question of whether a revolutionary can be a judge. My own reflection on Sachs has brought me to ask the additional question of whether a judge can be a revolutionary.[151] I end with Sachs:

> Looking back on my years on the Bench, then, I have no doubt that life experiences have entered into my legal consciousness in multiple ways, some very obvious and others quite mysterious. All have been integrated into and transformed by the legal culture in which my Court has operated. The little I can say with confidence is that our task has not been simply to try to solve problems through formal reasoning. Nor, on the other hand, has it merely been to wrap up purely personal preferences in legal vocabulary. Our judicial function has been to identify issues, to weigh the different considerations involved, to arrive at a proportionately balanced outcome that took account of the context and the constitutional values at stake and to share with the public all the reasoning that led to the final product. In a word, it has been to judge.[152]

Chapter 3

Interview with Emeritus Justice Albie Sachs

Drucilla Cornell and Karin van Marle

This is Drucilla Cornell, Karin van Marle, and Emeritus Justice Albie Sachs. Justice Sachs will be addressing a number of questions that have been formulated by Karin van Marle and myself as part of a book project and we are going to begin now. Today is August 2, 2011. We are at the University of Pretoria. It is now a shortly after 9 o'clock.

QUESTION (DRUCILLA): For all your life, prior to becoming a judge, you were a committed political activist. One particularly important aspect of your activism within the ANC was your work on the Code of Conduct for combatants in the struggle to overthrow apartheid. This was after Oliver Tambo had mentioned to you that some of the comrades in the ANC had engaged in torture against captured enemy agents. So we have two questions for you. Obviously you do not consider violence just a neutral mechanism that can be deployed to crush the enemy, but instead even an armed struggle must be conducted in accordance with the ideals that any particular movement is fighting for. What was it that inspired you to put those ideals into a written, even legalistic document, as a code of conduct? Secondly, I have suggested that we need a specific ideal of anti-violence which the French philosopher Étienne Balibar has called "civility," and which in South Africa we may identify as uBuntu, which in a certain sense goes beyond simply seeking consistency with the ideas the movement is fighting for, and actually makes anti-violence a key critical concept. Do you agree with the need for such a concept, whether we call it civility or uBuntu?

Albie: Is it permissible in the cause of an armed struggle for national liberation and democracy to use torture against captives sent to destroy your organization? This question underlays a request to me by Oliver Tambo, former law partner of Nelson Mandela, now leader of the ANC in exile, to help draft a Code of Conduct for the organization. The answer is not difficult, I told him: international legal instruments are very clear — no torture or inhuman or degrading treatment or punishment. He was quiet for a moment.

We use torture, he said. His face was bleak. I couldn't believe it. The ANC, the organization to which I belonged, body and soul, that was fighting for liberation, was using torture. Though I might have been a pacifist by temperament, I fully and unabashedly supported the right of the oppressed and disenfranchised majority to resort to armed struggle. But to counter violence with violence was one thing, to use torture was quite another.

For a long time our movement had in fact embraced non-violence as a cardinal principle of struggle.

My first serious political act was very much in the Gandhian non-violent tradition. A 17-year-old second-year law student in 1952, I led a small group of white volunteers to sit on post office seats marked non-whites only. Ten thousand black people had already taken part in the Defiance of Unjust Laws Campaign, expressly modeled on Gandhi's passive resistance struggles in South Africa. Volunteer-in-chief had been a lawyer in Johannesburg by the name of Nelson Mandela. The campaign was crushed, but the spirit of defiance continued, and three years later our movement adopted the Freedom Charter, opening with the words: "South Africa belongs to all who live in it, black and white." The state's response was the Treason Trial, in which 156 activists were indicted for trying to establish a non-racial democracy, which, the prosecution alleged — ironically echoing the unstated theoretical sentiments of the youth organization to which I belonged — could only be achieved by violence.

Called the Modern Youth Society, my organization had enthusiastically promoted the adoption of the Freedom Charter, evoking by its name the Chartist campaigns in Britain. Remember our struggle in South Africa was for the vote, not for independence — we sought universal franchise in a single, united country, rather than the creation of a separate state. Was it possible to follow the largely non-violent path of Britain, where, under pressure from the Chartist movement, the franchise had been progressively extended to include the workers and the poor (and eventually, women)? In our hearts we were unconvinced. The white supremacist foundation of the Union was profoundly oppressive. Without political self-determination for the dominated majority, individual human rights, including the vote, could never be meaningfully achieved. We firmly believed that what you now call Balibar's anti-violence principle could never operate in our country, where the possibilities of open civilian discourse between equal voices were officially and ruthlessly suppressed.

Ours was far more than a struggle for civil rights within the existing constitutional order with a view to making the Union of South Africa more perfect. As I was to write later, the achievement of civil rights would not be the instrument of our struggle, but its consequence ("Sovereignty is the essence, national liberation the substance, democracy the form and human rights the goal"). We accordingly envisaged achieving votes for all through a struggle for national liberation. And many of us dreamed of becoming armed combatants in that struggle.

We sang songs of the International Brigade in the Spanish Civil War, as well as the songs of struggle of Pete Seeger and Paul Robeson in the USA. The anti-Nazi partisans of Europe as well as the guerillas who fought in the Chinese Revolution inspired my generation, just as the Russian Revolution had inspired my parents, and Cuba, Algeria, Vietnam, Guinea-Bissau, Angola, Mozambique, and Nicaragua were to inspire later ones. When the Vice President of the Chinese Supreme Court visited the Constitutional Court of South Africa about five years ago, he was amazed to hear me sing a song which I had learnt from a Paul Robeson record — the Chinese National Anthem! My colleagues were also amazed and amused.

During those years I envisaged myself going up into the mountains and being part of an armed freedom struggle. I used to, for fun, climb Table Mountain every Sunday, and I'd come crazily running down, so fast that if I tripped, I could have broken my legs, even smashed my skull. But while enjoying the thrills of using gravity to hurtle down at breakneck speed, I didn't realize that I was straining the ligaments in my knees and destroying any chance of ever becoming a guerilla. To my utter dismay, I discovered that after a day's walk my knees would conk in. So, for eminently non-ideological reasons, my career as an armed combatant was over before it had even started.

In the end, the issue of whether to begin an armed struggle was effectively determined not by theoretical analysis, but by actions of the South African Government. Repression was getting worse, and even the limited scope for protest which we had had in the fifties, was denied. Organizations were banned, newspapers were banned, individuals were banned. There was one last attempt by Nelson Mandela in May 1961 to get a national convention to discuss a new constitution for South Africa. But the only response from the South African state was to intensify its efforts to capture him and to display the full power of its military might. And at the end of the year, the first bombs went off.

Although I myself never trained as a guerilla or carried a gun, I intellectually supported the armed struggle. Members of my youth movement bore arms and spent years in jail — George Peake five, Ben Turok two, Joseph Morolong five, Denis Goldberg 23. Basil February died in action. I have no doubt that focused and proportionate violence was a necessary ingredient of the freedom struggle. And even if ultimately we did not seize power as we had envisaged and instead negotiated the revolution, the willingness of some to give their lives for the freedom of all undoubtedly transformed the level of resistance and contributed massively to the liberation of our country.

The next moment of importance for these musings on non-violence recurred while I was an exile in London. It was around 1967, when an older comrade who had fought against Hitler in the Second World War, Wolfie Kodesh, said: "Albie, you've got to come to Peace House, there's a big meeting and Oliver Tambo is going to speak there this afternoon." Wolfie loved having a secret, but also loved people to know he had a secret. I went to Peace House wondering what it was all about. There were a few hundred people there, and Oliver Tambo comes up onto the stage and we stand up and sing freedom songs. We sit down expectantly. In a solemn voice he reads a formal announcement on behalf of the national executive of the ANC: "On such and such a date" — I am paraphrasing now — "the Luthuli detachment of Umkhonto we Sizwe [MK] entered the territory of [what was then called] Rhodesia, on its way to pursue the freedom struggle in South Africa. Their movements were betrayed, and the enemy forces of the Smith regime engaged them in fierce combat. The battle lasted for several hours, and at its end, five of the enemy soldiers lay dead on the ground, while not one of our combatants was injured." We stood up and we cheered. At last, at last, at last, we were fighting back! A breakthrough . . . And a voice from just behind where I was sitting, a very eloquent, very English voice, shouted out: "That's murder!"

We were shocked. "Who was this provocateur?" He shouted out again in his rather posh voice, "That's murder!" We were waiting for Oliver Tambo to hit back, to tell this interloper at our meeting that for decades it had always been our people who had lain bleeding on the field, that we had been denied any rights whatsoever, that conditions for the disenfranchised were getting worse. Instead, he stepped aside, thought for a moment, and said quietly: "Yes, we've become killers." He then went on in a soft voice to add that one of the worst things that apartheid had done had been to make it necessary for our young people, who would otherwise be building up the country, to take up arms and learn how to kill their fellow human beings.

I was stunned. And very moved, deeply moved. Maybe other people at the meeting don't even remember his reply, but I recall vividly how profoundly his message touched me. And looking back I can see how well it fitted in with the anti-violence foundation to the launching of the armed struggle. Killing might have become unavoidable, but it was never glorious; terrorism aimed at civilian targets should never be used, and the violence should be suspended as soon as serious and principled talking about how to achieve a non-racial democracy got under way.

To return to the question of torture. In a poem entitled "When bullets begin to flower," a Mozambican combatant had written: "It's not enough that our cause be pure and just; purity and justice must exist inside ourselves." War by its very nature sprang from human failure, employed brutal means, and relied on secrecy and deception for its success. Its objective was to conquer through superior might rather than convince through greater reasons; to break the will of the enemy rather than create a shared space for respectful dialogue between contending communities. In our case, the fact that we had been driven to resort to armed struggle did not mean that any form of violence whatsoever could be unleashed. All was *not* fair in love and revolution. The fact that a war was justified didn't mean that the way it was conducted was just. Central to our endeavor was our emancipatory vision.

People joining the resistance to apartheid brought in with them a variety of emotions — pain, rage, ambition, hope. We came from the most diverse backgrounds. What united us was shared hope and determination. The leadership constantly stressed — in word and deed — that the goal was not simply to destroy an evil system and seize the reins of power. It was to liberate our country, and all the people in it. Indeed, even the oppressors had to be freed from their narrowness, greed, and fear, and enabled to discover the humanity they had suppressed in themselves. Individuals like Nelson Mandela and Desmond Tutu have justly been honored for the manner in which they personally lived, and the values of human emancipation they articulated. But they did not invent the vision. Rather, they represented in particularly eloquent manner a culture of openness, hope, and humanity, one that had been forged by the experiences and interactions of millions of people in the course of the struggle. So in the course of doing underground work, people of the most diverse backgrounds learned to trust each other and share hope. Some came from comfortable homes. Many more lived in overcrowded shacks. Educational and linguistic gaps could be huge. But somehow the bonds became particularly strong because there was not obvious conformity of life experience, interests, and outlook. What united us was the purity of our idealism, coupled with the intensity of the risks we took and the arduous nature of the tasks we jointly undertook to achieve a common goal.

Central to the project was imagining and fighting for a better world, not only for ourselves, but for all humanity. I knew intuitively while Oliver Tambo spoke to me about the Code of Conduct, that if we resorted to the arbitrariness and cruelty of those we were fighting against, the main casualty would not be the enemy, but the organic solidarity that kept us all together.

Oliver Tambo mentioned to me the difficulties that the movement faced dealing with captured enemy agents, whose objectives were to destroy the organization, to carry out assassinations, to sabotage equipment. These activities were not the result of dissidence inside the organization, but part of the enemy's attacks on us. Host countries in Africa didn't want to be saddled with the problems of the different freedom movements — each exiled organization had to make its own arrangements. And it was clear to me that he, Oliver Tambo, supported the international principles as a lawyer, but not only as lawyer, but also as a person, as a leader, and as a Christian. His Christianity was very deep, and he often considered leaving the political struggle to become a full-time Anglican minister of religion.

So I had to find the language, the legal language, to crystallize an ideal of justice inside our own ranks, one that would be manageable and that would inspire the rank and file inside the ANC. At one stage in Maputo — remember I was not part of the MK — I had bumped into this man, we never asked for names, who asked me out of the blue: "Tell me comrade Albie, when you join the ANC, do you have any rights?" Now, I had never heard that question asked before. Lawyers like myself raised this kind of jurisprudential issue in class, but here was an MK soldier posing the question. When you joined the ANC voluntarily, dedicating your life to the collective freedom struggle, did you cede your right to have personal rights?

Oliver Tambo was never one to issue a decree from the top. He insisted that the issue of treatment of captives be dealt with in a democratic manner at a delegates conference, and be discussed in advance by the whole movement. In the result, the question of whether it was legitimate to use torture, or whatever euphemism was used, against captured enemy agents whose objective was to destroy the organization, and who might have important information about impending enemy action, was a deep matter of struggle morality. We discussed it in our different branches throughout the world.

I was then asked at an ANC conference in a small Zambian town, called Kabwe, to introduce the Code of Conduct. It operated at three levels. At the lowest level, it dealt with the legal processes to be followed in the case of people who came drunk to branch meetings and who were just disruptive, and so on. You dealt with that politically. The next level related to people who stabbed, stole, assaulted, crashed motorcars, and drove while drunk. We developed regional tribunals with a limited range of penalties to handle these alleged offenders. At the highest level, the Code of Conduct dealt with grave offences that were aimed at destroying the organization. These included killing members, assassinating leaders, using bombs and poison to cause mayhem. In dealing with these issues, very special procedures were laid down. Offences were defined with some precision. Evidence had to be led, and could be challenged. Defenders were provided. A range of permissible punishments was provided. There was a system of appeal. I think it is the most important legal work I've ever done.

The Code of Conduct could not of itself end all ill-treatment, but by introducing concepts of legality during the struggle, it undoubtedly helped bring about a major transformation of a liberation movement in exile. This legality was based not simply on political consciousness, but on rules, principles, and institutional mechanisms. You could not simply copy a court system presupposing that you have prisons, trained judges, procedures for appeal, and an apparatus for implementing legal orders. We had to invent something that would be rooted in our circumstances, but at the same time embody the values of fairness and humanity that lay at the heart of our struggle. As always, idealism and practicality went hand in hand. We wanted a functional set of rules that would give people confidence in the structures of the movement. The Code of Conduct was designed to help overcome arbitrariness, and develop a comradely sense of trust. Members would know there were established mechanisms to deal with problems and disputes. Your fate did not depend on the mood or whims of individuals.

At any event, in a hall surrounded by Zambian troops in case there would be commando raids to take out the 200 or so delegates of the ANC, we set aside a whole day to discussing the statutes of the ANC and the Code of

Conduct. It soon became clear that the only contentious issue was the question of whether in extreme situations it was permissible to use what were called "intensive methods of interrogation." Amongst the first speakers were two young soldiers in MK. I remember well the first one climbing up the steep steps to the microphone. He was brief and emphatic: "If you gave just the tiniest bit of leeway to security," he said, "they would never stop there — there must be no torture, full stop." Then the second man ascended: "We are fighting for life. How can we be against life?" To me, that captured everything. I was stirred. It was easy for me, the white lawyer growing up in relatively comfortable circumstances, to be motivated by the principles that we had learned in law school about what was right and fair. Here was this man from a generation of MK people fighting against enormous odds and difficulties. He is insisting on maintaining the principle that we were fighting for life, so that we could not be against life. The chances are that he did not survive the combat operations he later undertook. But his words might have been as important as any bullets he fired. The conference unanimously accepted that no exceptions would be allowed to the unqualified prohibition of torture or other forms of ill-treatment.

What emerges from these lengthy recollections is that it wasn't a purely personal matter for an individual named Albie Sachs to introduce these notions into the ANC. Nor was my motivation that I had read books of philosophy or been inspired by certain jurisprudential principles or values. In fact, I had never read Immanuel Kant then, just as I am being introduced to Balibar for the first time today by yourself. Not that we were disdainful of philosophical notions. In my youth movement we took political philosophy very seriously. We all wanted to study Marxism. But it was dangerous to do so — if caught we could go to jail for 10 years. So we hit on the idea of having a study class on political philosophy that would start with the ancient Greeks and only incidentally include Marx along the way. The trouble began with the pre-Socratics, who were so interesting that we needed two sessions on them alone. Then we dealt in turn with Socrates, Plato and Aristotle ... we never even reached the medieval philosophers, let alone Hegel, whom we were going to "stand on his head" to reach Marx and Engels! And far from embracing the pure, categorical, and enlightened reasoning of Kant, I ended up being immersed in the notion of the dialectic, of the impermanence of propositions, of the ever-evolving contradictions that lie at the heart of life as they lurk at the centre of the search for truth, as strongly emphasized by the pre-Socratics!

Thinking back to those times reminds me of how violent I suddenly discovered the state to be. The only violence I had personally known had come from tackling and being tackled on the rugby field. Now, locked in solitary confinement in police cells, I found myself in a world suffused with violence. My only connection with anything outside my cell was through sound. I could hear everything, from clanging doors to commands shouted out, and people screaming and banging, terrified. My ears burned with the horrible sound of a person locked up in the night and screaming and screaming and banging and banging, in rage and then going quiet for a few minutes, before the rage and banging start again. It brought home to me how much the state depends upon force, on subordinating the will of people subject to it.

For most poor people throughout the world, and people generally belonging to oppressed and marginalized groups, the law comes to them in violent form. It bullies and beats far more than it protects them. The second police station in which I was held was attached to a court. Every afternoon, Monday to Friday, I would hear kids being whipped, I could not see them. I could just hear them screaming . . . the first cry and then the second and up to the sixth . . . The screams would get wilder and wilder. That was when I really felt the sense of the state literally being an instrument of physical brutality. I recalled study classes I had conducted clandestinely at night in shacks with people willing to give their lives for justice and freedom. Their vitality, human energy, and belief in justice had been fantastic. But for them the law was not their protector. The law was the police demanding that they show their passes, the vans that were always on top of them, the police who would storm into their houses at any hour of the day or night. It was the law that allowed them to be locked up because they had not paid their debts. They ran from the law. The law was always pursuing them.

Only when it came to writing the new Constitution did the law being to offer real hope to the despised and rejected! It now expressly laid claim to being a humane engine of fairness and justice actively enhancing the dignity of those who had historically and systematically been oppressed and disadvantaged. The emancipatory vision of struggle was now converted into the transformatory vision of constitutional rights. And the process of achieving a national compact on what the foundation of rights in our fractured and fragmented society should be became the greatest guarantor of the sustainability of the constitutional project. To be honest, the constitution-making process was bumpy. There were massacres, breakdowns, mass actions, and threats of civil war. An armored car crashed into the building where negotiations were being conducted. The immensely popular Chris Hani, who had survived three assassination attempts during his years as an MK commander, was gunned down as he returned home from jogging. Even as the first democratic elections were held, bombs went off, killing several first-time voters. Yet despite these immense problems, a strong sense of security came from the very fact that former enemies could sit round a table, look into each other's eyes, and eventually come up with principled and workable solutions. Suddenly, dialogue between equals became the order of the day. Civility became king/queen. The Balibarian notion became feasible.

I stress the spirit of civility rather than the spirit of compromise. You can't compromise on some things, like having just a little bit of apartheid, or a little bit of capital punishment, or a little bit of torture. And in a broad sense you can't compromise on the basic democratic nature of the new society, or on the need to outlaw abusive use of state power, protect fundamental rights and prohibit unfair discrimination. You can have a degree of give-and-take on the best processes to follow with regard to accomplishing the necessary transformations, particularly in the transitional period. And there is always scope for meaningful debate on nuance and detail. But the great breakthroughs in our constitution-making process were not achieved by compromise, but by accommodation.

Compromise in this context implies a self-serving deal between political elites based on a shared interest in dividing the spoils of office. Accommodation presupposes going out of your way to understand and acknowledge the key preoccupations of other protagonists. Accommodation means understanding the viewpoints of others, their concerns, as well as respecting their dignity. Even if their concerns arise out of hateful circumstances that they themselves have created, and their fear is the fear of the oppressors who now have to relinquish their instruments of command, even then they are still human beings, they are part of the new nation. Thus, the project is to allow people to escape from or transcend all modes of oppressive behavior. We had to eschew the notion of: it was once their turn, now it is our turn. For us, the struggle for freedom meant getting beyond the idea that the only way forward for the oppressed people was to become oppressors themselves. In that sense our constitutional order was created through dialogue, civility, listening, understanding, and acknowledging the diversity amongst our people. The significance of diversity for citizenship lies not just in the rights that you have that cannot be violated whoever you are. Diversity is actually constitutive of the very idea of the new society where values that are oppressive to others have to be restrained, and appropriately so. The very pride of the country comes from the fact that accepting rather than suppressing difference, we achieved what many had thought to be impossible, a common citizenship based on securing equality of fundamental rights for all.

And the person who was the absolute exemplar in promoting unity in diversity was Oliver Tambo. Working with him was especially moving for me because we came from very different backgrounds. He grew up in a deep rural area, whereas I came from a cosmopolitan urban background. He was strongly imbued with an African nationalist patriotism, whereas from infancy I had grown up in an atmosphere of internationalism. He was a deeply committed Christian, while I was from a totally secular home. You would have wondered what we could have had in common at all. Well, to begin with, we were both what I would call "soft" people who had found themselves in a hard struggle, he as a leader, I as a member. I think, by the way, that freedom struggles need "hard" people and they need soft people — if you have too many of one or the other it can be dangerous. He had a gentleness, a reflectiveness, and a kind of spirituality to which I responded. I like to think he found something of a similar resonance in me as well. Once, when he went to attend a world conference on religion in London — he was very apologetic about even going there — he asked me, a person who was as deeply non-religious as he was deeply religious, to help prepare his speech. The ANC had a religious desk, which could advise him on how to win over Catholic, or Jewish or Muslim or Methodist leaders. But he wanted something deeper, more profound, concepts that dealt with issues of deep conscience, formulations that evoked a sense of intense humanity and human solidarity, that transcended race, sect, gender, birth, culture, and station, ideas that respected people for who they were.

We have many traditions in our country, not all of them good. There is a tradition in the ANC, not always lived up to, of democratic discussion. This culture is relevant to the role of civility and democracy, which is touched on in your question here. Of inestimable value has been the tradition of honest, open debate right at the heart of struggle. Indeed, the more intense the issue, the more that turned on decisions to be made, the more important was free, candid, and principled debate. Oliver Tambo was a great listener, a natural democrat, always diplomatic in speech and demeanor, but never afraid to deal with hard and testing questions. Many other liberation movements in exile fragmented, fractured, formed splinter groups, and expelled and even killed each other. Yet over a period of 30 years in which he led the movement in exile, I can only recall 10 members being expelled from the ANC, eight on one occasion, and two or three on another. This had a lot to do with his style of leadership, a culture that he had helped develop when he had worked under the Presidency of Chief Albert Luthuli.

QUESTION (DRUCILLA): In a recent panel in the uBuntu Project, Emeritus Justice Laurie Ackerman described you as a man of extraordinary commitment to ideals and great material courage. In a time in which ideals are often condemned as the legacy of a defeated revolutionary tradition, how do you currently defend your own idealism for which you were willing to risk your life? There is an existential dimension to this question, which is that as a young man you thought that part of the meaning of life was to have ideals that were important enough to risk your life for. How do you answer the cynics who simply reject idealism? Further, how do you answer those more sophisticated critics who argue that all ideals are "bad" idealizations in the Freudian sense, in that they underpin self-righteous fantasies that often lead the idealist to engage in forms of social and political activity that seem to undermine the very ideals for which he or she stands. Simply put: can one be an idealist and avoid self-righteousness?

Albie: The first judgments the new Constitutional Court gave included decisions outlawing capital punishment and corporal punishment by the state. Nelson Mandela, who had nearly been hanged himself, sent Advocate

George Bizos to argue on behalf of the new government that capital punishment should be abolished. And so, what was an affirmative moment for me was a foundational moment for the Constitutional Court — it ruled against the death penalty in the name of the great ideals of the Bill of Rights.

The question is: How did it come about that I, Albie Sachs, having been part of a struggle that called itself revolutionary and was animated by certain world view, could come to the same position on capital punishment as Laurie Ackermann, who had never been part of that struggle? Indeed, Laurie Ackermann came to his anti-death penalty position through a very different rationality: Kantianism and Christian humanism. What does a good revolutionary do on a court with people who don't see themselves as good revolutionaries? Do I get into a corner and fight for my positions in my political language, using my vocabulary and points of reference? Did I say to my colleagues that it was my revolutionary commitment that motivated me in my judgments? Not at all. I did not want to do that. I did not feel that it was right to do that. I felt that the oath that I took to judge without fear, favor, or prejudice, to do justice to all according to the law and the Constitution, demanded an unmediated loyalty to the law and the Constitution.

This was not problematic. The Constitution embodied the very things we had been fighting for. It represented a continuation of, not a rupture, with my previous life. I did not feel that I was manacling myself to a set of abstract juridical principles alien to the ideals that had guided my life through prison, exile, statelessness, and losing an arm and sight of an eye to a bomb placed in my car. On the contrary, as I have written elsewhere, the achievement of constitutional democracy represented what I called my soft vengeance. It gave meaning to our trauma, validated our lives, and substantiated our idealism. My commitment to the Court, then, was not based on notions of revolutionary deployment. It was wholehearted, involving, enthusiastic participation in a new embodiment of the struggle for human dignity. The former intense comradeship based on political objectives now gave way to close collegiality derived from constitutional principles. In practice, then, vocabulary and structures of thought of an insurrectionary movement gave way seamlessly to the language of transformation and fundamental rights. The guiding constitutional principles of human dignity, equality, and freedom provided a robust existential bridge between the old political activism and the new judicial engagement.

Looked at from a subjective, personal point of view, I think three factors had facilitated my trajectory towards constitutionalism. The first was coming to terms with the concepts of pluralism and open democracy. While exiled in London, I had listened carefully to debates on Karl Popper's defense of an open society, and come away somewhat skeptical. But years later when I returned to South Africa my view had changed drastically.

In 1992, the Inaugural Lecture I gave as an honorary professor at the University of Cape Town was called "Perfectibility and corruptibility." Its basic notion was that all constitutions are based on containing and managing the tension between perfectibility and corruptibility. Perfectibility drew upon hope, idealism, and the expectation that people could live together with dignity, comfort, and honor. Corruptibility, on the other hand, stemmed from the capacity of all of us to do things that are wrong, and sometimes evil and cruel.

Many of my comrades and friends had been envisaging some kind of beautiful ideal society, spending all their adult lives preparing for the revolution that would bring it about. Now it seemed that the prospect of a revolution was being snatched away before their eyes. Instead, we were going to negotiate a new Constitution — the very thing that Mandela had called for 30 years earlier. It was not just his call that made me an ardent proponent of negotiations. It was the experience I had had of living in revolutionary Mozambique.

My arrival there was marvelous. We called it a liberated zone of humanity. This was the Revolution, and we were the beautiful people. The first Portuguese phrases I learned were about the emancipation of women, and the need to combat racialism, regionalism, and tribalism. Every single institution had a cultural unit that would organize choral singing and group dancing and put on plays. We painted murals on walls all over the city. Extraordinary work was being done in anthropology and archaeology. Recuperating African history by examining social structures and the lives of ordinary people, the researchers rejected the notion of a marvelous classless African past. Exploitation had existed since the earliest times, as if to underline just as exploitation was rampant in many countries in Africa today.

The battle-cry in the newly independent People's Republic was for reconstruction to further the interests of workers and peasants. The owners of beautiful high-rise apartments had fled and the balconies now contained the washing lines of people who had previously only entered as cleaners and cooks. A poem I wrote went more or less along the following lines, "Of all the banners in Maputo / of all the flags that fly / the ones that stir me most of all / are the clothing out to dry."

But along with other African countries, Mozambique paid a bitter price for supporting the struggle against apartheid. The combination of war and severe underdevelopment proved devastating. And all of the country's severe problems were compounded by what turned out to be serious errors of policy.

There was a poignant story about a discussion between Samora Machel and his father. In the colonial period, Samora's father had been expelled from a small piece of land along the Limpopo River to make way for Portuguese peasants to grow rice there. After Independence, the colonists returned to Portugal, and Papa Machel asked his son the President when he could start growing rice there again. To his dismay, and our delight, Samora replied that

FRELIMO had not been fighting for the President's father to get land, but for the nation to get food. With Bulgarian help, the FRELIMO Government created a huge state farm on the banks of the Limpopo. The tractors came to till the soil, but they put in too much fertilizer. The rice grew too quickly, and they had to get volunteers from the towns to cut the suddenly sprouting crop. I was part of a lorry-load. Now, if anybody asks me to come and cut rice, even if I still have two arms, you know they are in desperate straits. Vast sums of money went fruitlessly into the project. Our delight turned to dismay. The objective was beautiful, but the result was calamitous.

Perhaps the greatest lesson we South Africans who lived there learned was that there was a deep flaw at the heart of the country's political system — the absence of space for legitimate opposition. Suddenly, war raged everywhere. We heard the guns from across the bay, and refugees streamed in. After being the beautiful people in a beautiful country, filled with inspiration, we came to have thousands of persons like me without limbs; millions of refugees in neighboring countries; brother fighting brother, sister fighting sister.

Thus, by the time I returned to South Africa, I didn't regard the idea of a negotiated settlement as something forced on us because we weren't strong enough to seize power. It was, as Shakespeare says, "a consummation devoutly to be wished." A negotiated revolution would enable us to retain the physical fabric of the country. More importantly, it would prevent the terrible scarring and hatred that goes from generation to generation when you establish power against the will of another group. Furthermore, those who seize power don't have to think about the best forms of governing: you simply legitimize the government that you've installed, and then rely on the continuation of your power to stay in control.

The result was that at the negotiations I was the one who, with all the fervor of a convert, insisted on the word "open" being attached to the word "democratic" — what we envisaged was an open and democratic society. It was not enough just to have periodic elections — in addition channels of accountability, debate, and contestation should be kept open at all times. In the flavorful language of the US President Lyndon Johnson, rather have your opponents in the tent pissing out, than out of the tent pissing in.

The second important discovery for me came from attending an international conference with many participants who were fighting against military dictatorship in Latin America. They spoke about "derechos humanos" (human rights) with the same passion and commitment that we had when referring to national liberation. Much of the literature I read those days spoke dismissively about "so-called human rights." This cynicism was understandable at a time when US foreign policy denounced socially progressive governments for violating human rights, while simultaneously training assassins and torturers to overthrow those governments. The ardor of my companeros and companeras in defense of derechos humanos enabled me to abandon forever the tag "so-called." Human rights were human rights.

Once more, it was experience of struggle rather than conceptual analysis that brought home to me the indivisibility and overlap between sovereignty, national liberation, democracy, and human rights.

The third factor was of a different order. After decades of using all our energy in denunciation of a wicked and unjust system, it was wonderfully liberating to be able to express fully the nurturing, creative, and constructive side of our nature. In a way the great paradox of our lives was that we had expended all our passion to create a boring society. What we were doing on the Court lacked the grandeur and epic quality of the Revolution we had once envisaged. We did not have to be heroic any more to achieve the mundane decencies that every human being should be able to take for granted. But there was a moral texture to our work that flowed in an intensely practical form from the emancipatory vision that had brought us into struggle in the first place. If we no longer conceived of ourselves as the agents of historical necessity (freedom is the recognition of necessity — Frederick Engels), we were citizens consciously choosing to side with those promoting human dignity and reducing inhumanity and injustice in the world.

About a month ago, I attended a conference in Montreal to honor Charles Gonthier, a Canadian Supreme Court judge who died a couple of years back. Charles had come to the opening of our Court. We got on really well. A quiet, modest person, he was enthusiastic about our project in South Africa, even though he came from a faraway French-speaking, Catholic, family-oriented, and rather conservative community. His big theme was fraternity, and the conference to honor him was a conference on fraternity. In my address, I mentioned that his idea of fraternity was close to the Southern African notion of uBuntu.

I said I was drawn to travel all the way to Montreal precisely because Charles and I had been so different in world views, yet so firmly together in respect of our constitutional vision. What he called fraternity, I referred to as uBuntu. Yet whether expressed in French, or isiXhosa or English, or in a judgment of the Supreme Court of Canada or the Constitutional Court of South Africa, the basic understanding was the same: we are each unique individual human beings who live together in communities. I cannot separate my humanity from an acknowledgement of and appreciation of your humanity. The principles of liberty and equality are accordingly strengthened, not weakened, when integrated with the principle of fraternity (human solidarity, uBuntu). Interdependence enhances the unique quality and worth of each individual while enriching the texture and fabric of the community as a whole.

The only writer I know who has dealt directly with how it is possible for judges of widely different philosophical views to establish common constitutional ground is Cass Sunstein. He argues for under-theorization and a minimalist approach to achieve a degree of principled consensus in relation to such issues as when life support for irrecuperably brain-damaged persons should be withdrawn. I do not understand minimalism in this context to require judges to repudiate or deny the deep factors of life and professional experience that animate everything they do. Judges are not empty vessels, waiting to be filled with the noise of litigants. The fact that each judicial conscience should be robust and unique, however, does not mean that each judge should be wayward and idiosyncratic, allowing personal predilections and prejudices to determine outcomes. On the contrary, part of the resilience of the strong judicial conscience comes from its acknowledgment that it should not be overweening, that it should acknowledge the multitude of competing and coalescing belief systems that exist off and on the Bench, and that it should bend the knee, always and only, to the Constitution and the Law. Indeed, it is the refraction of everything through the constitutional prism that makes judicial life so strenuous and so interesting (and, at times, so lonely).

When the first judges on the Constitutional Court were sworn in, some of us said "So help me God," others merely affirmed; some were Christians, some came from Jewish or Muslim backgrounds; some were men, others women; we had able-bodied and disabled; some had been judges at the time of apartheid, others advocates, others law professors; some had been to jail or worked in the underground without being caught; some had belonged to the disenfranchised majority; others to the privileged minority; some were in their 60s, others in their 30s. To this day I don't know how my colleagues voted in elections, if they voted at all, or even what their favorite reading matter or movies or music was. What I do know is that all of them: firstly, detested apartheid and assumptions of racial or gender supremacy; secondly, believed wholeheartedly in the values of human dignity, equality and freedom set out in the Constitution; and, thirdly, accepted that the promise of the Constitution could not be realized without serious engagement with the unjust allocation of resources and life opportunities systematically created in the part.

Within that common frame we each had varied voices, body language, and writing styles. Laurie Ackermann occasionally referred expressly to Immanuel Kant as providing a profound philosophical justification for a proposition he adopted. I was able to concur even if I had not studied Kantian philosophy. What mattered was that I could accept the validity of the proposition on its own merits and in the context of the Laurie judgment, and do so as a colleague trusting the accuracy of the citation, without necessarily identifying myself as a disciple of Kant.

I do not understand minimalism to mean that all philosophical foundation is extruded from our judgments. I mean instead that the deep existential personal idiosyncratic factors that animate every human being, including judges, get filtered through a kind of refraction, a constitutional refraction. It is the sharing of this process of refraction that makes it possible for the atheist and the committed Christian, the Sufi person, and the African spiritualist, to work together on a court. By so doing, they are not denying their belief systems, or pretending to espouse beliefs that they do not have. They are enhancing a form of qualitative, deliberative judicial reasoning, based on respect for the 3Cs that should govern judicial activity: civility, collegiality, and courage.

Drucilla: You played a major role long before ascending to the position of Justice on the Constitutional Court, advocating that socioeconomic rights must be rendered enforceable, and not relegated to a category of right that is different from first generation rights like the right to free speech. Indeed, when you were working in Mozambique, you argued against those who opposed the Bill of Rights because they were concerned that rights would just re-inscribe inequality, on the basis of a much more expansive explanation of socioeconomic rights and what such an expansive notion of a Bill of Rights could achieve.

Albie: The big and undiscussed issue in the ANC during the whole revolutionary period of repression, exile, and revolt from 1960 to 1990 was people's power versus an open pluralist society. Central though the question was, I cannot recall a single overt discussion of it during those years. It was what we now call the elephant in the room. For Oliver Tambo, there was never any question that the ANC would stand firmly in favor of an open, pluralist society. He not only signed on to the Freedom Charter; he completely believed in it. I think he always hoped that we could have a relatively peaceful overthrow of apartheid and create a country based on unqualified equality and full democratic rights, without bantustans and white areas and black areas. He also believed in the open society and diversity of points of view, and that applied within the ANC itself as well. He often spoke of the ANC as the parliament of the people. As the President of the organization, he called for discipline and loyalty to its core values, without seeing to create a militarized, monolithic revolutionary organization that demanded obedience and top-down control. His philosophy was that all the basic problems of the ANC needed to be resolved by thoughtful decision-making by the organization as a whole. Every voice had to be heard. He listened to all and would be the last one to speak. Each year on January 8 he would make an official statement on behalf of the ANC. And on that date in 1986, I think, Oliver Tambo formally announced that the ANC accepted the vision of a multi-party democracy in South Africa. This did not envisage the seizing of power and then producing a constitution that solidified the new power and repressed the enemy. On the contrary, it presupposed that the notion of multi-partyism would be central to the process whereby apartheid was dismantled and democracy installed.

The strategic implications were important. If there were going to be negotiations, they would not be about a regime surrendering power and abandoning the country. On the contrary, those currently involved in racial domination would remain in the country, but be obliged to release their exclusive hold on the instruments of power, and run for office like the members of any other political group.

Then in the January 8 statement a year later, Oliver Tambo announced that the ANC accepted the inclusion in a new Constitution of a Bill of Rights entrenching fundamental rights for all. I didn't know what discussion preceded this announcement. But it became clear that just as we had long had the time of the soldier, we were now approaching the time of the lawyer. ANC supporters were all familiar with the Freedom Charter. But what was meant by a Bill of Rights? Not all of us had the same idea about what it meant.

A group of black students at the University of Natal had set up an anti-Bill of Rights committee. What, people from the oppressed community being against a Bill of Rights! They were worried that a Bill of Rights was being created in anticipation of majority rule one day, with a view to ensuring that the 87 percent of property [and probably 95 percent productive capital] which by law belonged to whites would be constitutionally frozen in white hands. They saw the Bill of Rights as a Bill of Whites. Their fears were well grounded, but not, I felt, their solution. It all depended on the Constitution that emerged, and the terms of the Bill of Rights it would contain. A Bill of Rights could block emancipation or promote emancipation. If ever I had doubted the importance of ideas and theorizing in the struggle for justice, now the role of concepts became absolutely clear.

I gave a public lecture in Mozambique on the Bill of Rights as an emancipatory document. There was no reason at all to hand over the concept of fundamental human rights to the intellectuals of the propertied and the privileged classes. I had read a paper on "The three generations of human rights" by a Czech citizen working for the United Nations. This was in the late 1970s, and the only way he could place green or environmental rights firmly on the agenda was to invent three generations of rights. In giving the rights' paradigm an evolutionary character, I am sure he did not contemplate the survival of the weakest to ensure, on the contrary, that green rights would end up having the same status as the right to vote and the right to eat.

That article inspired me to argue that we could not allow rights to be limited to the first generation of civil and political rights, important as they were. In fact, limiting the Bill of Rights to civil and political rights could result in constitutionalizing private apartheid. You could abolish all the racist state laws governing ownership and occupation on land, but freeze the status quo through freedom of association. This would enable neighborhoods to declare themselves for whites only, school communities to have schools for whites only. So it was necessary to turn the idea of the Bill of Rights around, from what could be seen as a weapon of exclusion and domination, to become an instrument of liberation and emancipation. And to do that, the Bill of Rights would have expressly to include socioeconomic rights.

Our rank and file supporters simply could not understand that the right to education could not be a fundamental right. And what could be more fundamental than the right to save your child from dying of preventable diseases, or hunger? To separate the mind, which makes choices, and the body, in which the mind exists, might be okay for people who take bodily comfort for granted. After all, if you live in a beautiful house and have access to schooling and medical care, you don't need access to housing, health, or education — your money does the trick. But if you lack all these, and have been deprived of land, skills, and employment, your dignity as a human being requires that they progressively be made available to you.

At the same time, the placing of social and economic rights firmly on the agenda should not be allowed to serve as an excuse for discarding or subordinating civil and political rights. On the contrary, the Bill of Rights, like the Universal Declaration and the Freedom Charter, should protect multi-party democracy, the right to vote, and freedom of speech with the same commitment it showed to realizing access to health, housing, and education.

I recently saw a film that included a portion of a presentation I made to an ANC workshop in Lusaka. I looked so earnest, I still had two arms. It was a few weeks before the bomb went off in my car. My task was to explain why we supported a Bill of Rights, and my heart was racing. The first two reasons were straightforward enough. At a tactical level we needed to show the world that we were fighting to achieve freedom for all, and not to create a new form of dictatorship. Strategically — and this was Oliver Tambo's crucial contribution to the debate raging over a new constitutional dispensation for our country — a Bill of Rights protecting the fundamental rights of all, was the ANC's answer to claims that special protections for whites should be built into the new constitutional structures. Even our friends internationally were urging us to be realistic and provide such racially based guarantees. What a disaster that would have been. Instead of the Constitution being seen as embodying an emancipatory vision that would serve as the foundation for respecting diversity in a unified country, it would have been regarded by the majority of citizens as a mechanism for preserving racial privilege. So we refused to get real, and remained ideal! As it turned out, the adoption of that principled standpoint, far more than the personality of certain leaders, became the foundation of what came to be called the South African miracle.

At any rate, explaining the diplomatic and strategic reasons for having a Bill of Rights was the easy part of the presentation. The third aspect related to considerations of a more difficult nature — it was to tell the delegates that we needed a Bill of Rights against ourselves. When I told the participants that we had all lived in countries where leaders who had fought bravely for freedom had gone on to become authoritarian rulers themselves, I was nervous. Some of these countries were hosting our movement and giving us significant moral and material support. Many were paying a heavy price in blood for doing so. Once again, I was wondering if there would be objection to a lawyer from a privileged background throwing doubt on how unwavering the organization's commitment would be to the principles inscribed on its banner. And once again I discovered that candor in defense of a clearly stated and time-honored major principle was appreciated, not despised. Indeed, I sensed a feeling of relief, even delight, in the eyes of the participants. Though all would have felt overwhelming pride in the organization, everyone knew of abuses that had happened it its ranks and wrong things that had been committed in its name. Often in moments of disappointment I would console myself with the thought that the whole was greater than the parts.

So there was a general consensus that we needed to submit ourselves to the moral and practical discipline of an entrenched Bill of Rights. And so it came about that when we set out our vision for a future Constitution, both formal freedoms and socio-economic rights were included, on the understanding that each would reinforce the other.

QUESTION (DRUCILLA): In the years before you retired from the bench, you became a leader in the development of uBuntu jurisprudence. Both in terms of socioeconomic rights, but also as in areas of the private law, such as *delict*. Could you explain how you came to understand uBuntu both as an important ethical ideal of the majority population, and as a judicial principle? You have long been an advocate of how crucial it is in South Africa to incorporate the majority views of South Africa, but do you believe that that is the only work that uBuntu can do? Or do you think it applies more broadly to socioeconomic rights, here specifically I am thinking of *Port Elizabeth*. Like many others who were on the Constitutional Court during the first 15 years, you seemed to accept that South Africa is a *Rechtsstaat*, and a *Rechtsstaat* in your own judgments takes what Étienne Balibar calls "equaliberty" very seriously. The state not only can, but has an obligation to, regulate civil society in accordance with the ideals of a constitution. Obviously in *Port Elizabeth*, you developed uBuntu as a way of thinking about how to negotiate the conflict between the right of private property and the right to have a house. How far do you think the state can go in regulating economic relations we associate with advanced capitalist society in order to move toward a social order in which there is significantly less inequality? This question has both an institutional and philosophical and jurisprudential aspect. The first is: how far can the Constitutional Court go as a court? For example, in socioeconomic rights, in moving the society away from conventional notions of capitalist relations of production, obviously rooted in the right of private property and the free movement of capital. The second question is how far Parliament can — or should — go in regulating those relations? These jurisprudential questions take us back to your response to the anti-anti-Bill of Rights Advocates, and a conventional Marxist critique of rights, which you obviously reject. What is and can be the material efficacy of rights, and the Bill of Rights itself, in moving society toward a more egalitarian one than currently exists in South Africa. For you, clearly, the Bill of Rights is not simply a superstructure that ideologically

justifies advanced capitalism, but rather has a material force in that it embodies and enforces ideals.

Albie: These are very direct questions, to which I will give very indirect responses. Let me start with one of the most amusing moments in my 15 years on the Court, which occurred when I tried to find a word that described rule by judges. The term "juristocracy" worried the fussy part of me — it combined a Latin beginning with a Greek ending! Tut, tut. So I asked George Bizos, a legal friend of Greek origin, what the Greek word for judge was, and he told me it was dikos. The term dikocracy somehow did not seem appropriate. Indeed, he answered, but one could use the broader word dikastos. And so George and I cobbled together the term "dikastocracy." The point was to establish that the Constitution did not create a dikastocracy, that is, a system in terms of which a group of enlightened judges would determine the basic social and economic structures of society. This is not to say that judges had no role to play in bringing about social and economic transformation. On the contrary, no jurisprudence of rights would have any meaning if it did not grapple with the deeply entrenched and systemic inequalities left behind by centuries of colonialism and apartheid. The Constitution itself was explicitly transformative in this respect. It spoke of the *establishment* of social justice and the *achievement* of a non-racial and non-sexist society. It contained a strong and comprehensive equality clause, coupled with authorization of programs to redress past disadvantage. In addition, it guaranteed rights of workers to fair labor practices, form unions, and bargain collectively. It provided for restitution of land to people dispossessed by racist laws and practices, and facilitated upgrading of land tenure rights and the achievement of land reform. And, of course, the progressive realization of social and economic rights was explicitly mandated.

Then to my mind equally important, the Constitution provided a whole range of institutional processes which could be used by marginalized and impoverished groups to secure better lives for themselves. These included not only entrenched rights of expression, movement, political mobilization, voting, and standing for office. They covered the right to information and the right to just administrative action. Thus, considerable space was guaranteed to social movements that wished to campaign for radical social change of the kind envisaged in the question you put to me. And in more general terms, the Court went on to emphasize that the Constitution was based on principles of participatory democracy that required a degree of public involvement in the legislative process that went beyond simply taking part in elections and speaking to portfolio committees in Parliament.

The Constitutional Court has, I believe, tried assiduously to function within the letter and the spirit of the Constitution's transformatory agenda. In one case, it refused an invitation to approach regulation of betting on horses, on the basis that the starting-off point of the analysis must be a constitutional right to free enterprise. Similarly, though many of us on the Court might have favored decriminalization of sex work/prostitution, we could not hold that open and democratic societies recognized the commercialization of sex as a fundamental right that could not be regulated by the state. Conversely, however, the Court declined to accept a forcefully presented argument by Professor Dennis Davis that it should move its equality jurisprudence away from a focus on removing impediments to the enjoyment of human dignity, toward a concentration on achieving greater material equality. The fact is that while many freedoms, including the right to pursue a vocation, are clearly enshrined and have to be protected, no particular economic system is either required or endorsed by the Constitution. At the same time, any government, whether calling itself capitalist or socialist, would, however, have to work within the normative framework of rights and responsibilities established by the preamble, foundational principles, and Bill of Rights in the Constitution.

Once upon a time it all seemed so simple — government was part of a superstructure reflected and reinforced the economic base of society. Then, for those of us living in exile in London, along came two English intellectuals who messed everything up. The first was E. P. Thompson, the radical social historian, who said that through the ages the poor and oppressed had invoked concepts such as the right to justice and the rule of law in their struggles to mitigate the ravages of class oppression. Later, Ralph Milliband of the LSE had thrown a cat among the theoretical pigeons by arguing that far from the state simply being an instrument of ruling class domination, the state itself became part of the terrain of struggle (this notion was later extended to international financial institutions — friends of mine joined the World Bank as a terrain of struggle!). Oh for a return to the days when, in the words of Roberto Unger, we saw ourselves as revolutionaries acting as agents of historical necessity. I remember how much I had hated the poem of Gerald Manley Hopkins: "Glory be to God for Dappled Things." This was not because of his invocation of the Deity, but because of his praise of ambiguity and uncertainty. Now, decades later, I had become a dappled thing myself. Instead of using my endeavors to smite reactionaries, I was a samurai for a vague thing called justice, employing even vaguer weapons like values, context, impact, and proportionality.

Yet, looking back at the work we did on the Court, I see a clear continuity with the basic emancipatory impulses that had thrust many of us into the struggle in the first place. We delivered judgments to eliminate brutal forms of punishment; to promote participatory democracy; to achieve rights and freedoms for women; recognize indigenous land rights; to protect the rights of the child; to advance the rights of sexual minorities; to enable prisoners to vote; to provide access to anti-retroviral medication for persons living with HIV; to ensure that workers would not be unfairly dismissed and that the homeless would not be unjustly evicted. Much of the work of the Court was concerned with moving our society away from what Etienne Mureinik called a culture of authority to a culture of justification. We defended free speech, a right to just administrative action, a right to information, and a right to open justice. Civil society organizations and NGOs regularly came to our Court to pursue claims on behalf of the marginalized and the poor, to protect the environment, and to ensure justice for people living with HIV.

It was fortuitous but symbolically apt that the last case heard by the last four surviving founding members of the Court concerned the constitutionality of the provision of latrines for use by a community living in shacks not far from the Court. The inhabitants who had come to the Court heard counsel for the state open with an apology to the Court for the unacceptable delay by the authorities in providing promised brick houses with appropriate sewage. Dikgang Moseneke, the Deputy Chief Justice who was presiding, and who had earned his law degree while serving a 10-year prison sentence on Robben Island, told counsel he should apologize to the inhabitants, not to the Court. The apology was duly delivered, and received with evident appreciation. In the end, given the imminence of new housing, we did not feel it would be reasonable to order the VIPs (ventilated improved pit latrines) the inhabitants were seeking. But the litigation had in fact advanced the date when the houses would be delivered, and the inhabitants had had a meaningful day in which their concerns were seriously discussed by the highest authority in the land.

Drucilla: If I could just push you a bit on another dimension in the *Port Elizabeth* judgment. I want to return to something you've said over and over again about the importance of mutual recognition of the humanity and citizenship of others as a way of mediating the entire conflict between property owners and shanty-dwellers. In the United States, the only question that would be asked is: are you illegally on property, and if the answer is yes, then you can be evicted. So there is a narrative that goes with *Port Elizabeth* that whether or not you are illegally on private property cannot resolve the question, because citizens in the new South Africa must be willing to understand that this Bill of Rights is only as good as the willingness to respect the humanity of all other citizens. So I would like you to speak a bit about the role of mediation in eviction cases, and how you associate mediation with uBuntu in the *Port Elizabeth* case.

Albie: I think the word "narrative" is important here, a theme that is often underplayed in jurisprudential analysis. The *Port Elizabeth* case actually caused a personal crisis in my life. I feared that I might have to resign from the Court because I might find myself unable to honor my oath to do justice to all without fear, favor, or prejudice according to the law. Fifteen or so African families were living in shacks that they had built on vacant land owned by white families occupying elegant homes nearby. Clearly the occupation by the shack-dwellers was unlawful — you cannot just go and put up your shack on somebody else's land. But how could I, who had been committed to the freedom struggle all my life, order them to give up the only homes they had on earth? Happily, I was able to transform a personal crisis into an intellectual dilemma. Our constitutional rights were in conflict. The one upheld the right not to be arbitrarily deprived of property. The other gave everyone the right of access to adequate housing, and the right not to be evicted from their home except by an order of a court that took account of all relevant circumstances. A statute went on to provide further that the court should only order an eviction if it was just and equitable to do so. My moral dilemma therefore translated into a legal conundrum: what would be just to the landowners, whose property had been invaded, would not be equitable to the shack-dwellers, whose homes would be demolished, and, of course, vice versa.

It soon became clear that simply applying the technical rules of land law could not resolve the dilemma. All of us knew why desperate homeless people put up their shacks on the property of others. In our country dispossession, not possession, was quite literally nine points of the law (almost literally so: as a result of colonial conquest and successive land statutes, 87 percent of the surface area of the country had been reserved for exclusive white ownership). Historical and moral factors were clearly integral to any purely legal narrative seeking to decide what was just and equitable. And the story told in the judgment had used judicial language that was both so coherent and accessible that anyone reading it would say: yes, of course, that's why we have a Constitution, yes, of course, all fair-minded readers will agree that justice and equity must take account of the historical connection between race, landlessness, and homelessness, and yes, of course, it was incontestable that the injustice of the reality lived by millions had to be embodied in the process of deciding what was just and equitable.

At the same time, a countervailing story had to be told. In a constitutional state, the answer to injustice could not lie in arbitrary land invasions and opportunistic self-help. To do justice, then, the Court could not follow the common law rules of land law, in a technical, formalistic, and de-contextualized way, using classification and definitional reasoning to decide who was in the right. Nor, on the other hand, could it rely simply on the subjective emotions of individual judges to rectify past wrongs. Rather, the Court was called upon to function in a new manner, namely, to manage a stressful social process in a principled and fair way, taking account of the constitutional values involved. This is where the procedural remedy of mediation came to be invoked. Justice and equity required through mediation that the parties engage meaningfully with each other before eviction could be granted. Mediation did more than offer the possibilities of finding practical ways of minimizing hardship and inconvenience. It brought the parties into direct relationship with each other, something that had been impossible in the land of apartheid, that is, of enforced separation and division, and something that had now become integral to the new notion of shared citizenship. In a sense, the right to be taken seriously and to be listened to is foundational to the exercise of all rights.

To summarize: the connection between the whites living in a very up-market suburb nearby, and the impoverished black families living in the shacks, could not be established purely through observing the technicalities of land law. As citizens of the new non-racial democracy, all were now inhabitants of the same political community. Those who had in fact received historical advantages and those who had been disadvantaged were now literally neighbors. The nation-building, as you call it, that we hoped to achieve with the Bill of Rights, demanded that we acknowledge the humanity and citizenship of others, and each take responsibility for the other. The judgment pointed out the fact that in a relatively wealthy country millions of our people were living in self-made shacks was an assault not only on the dignity of the homeless, but on the dignity of all of us. As judges applying the Bill of Rights we had to respond to the constitutional imperative to humanize our society and civilize relationships. The Constitution envisaged restoring dignified connections between the advantaged and the disadvantaged, the rich and the poor. It was this effort to civilize our people and restore human connection that I came to associate with uBuntu. The judgment accordingly stated that the Bill of Rights was nothing if not uBuntu writ large.

I can recall, as I'm sure you can, Drucilla, that at a conference some time before that, you had asked me whether I saw uBuntu as an operative constitutional principle. And much to your dismay, I had said no. At that time I understood uBuntu as a value that informed the operation of constitutional principles, but not as a constitutional value with operative force itself. Maybe I had to wait for the right case to rethink uBuntu. It emerged as a core operational principle that tied together the notions of human dignity, freedom, and equality. It went to the heart of interpreting the Bill of Rights. The *Port Elizabeth Municipality* matter turned out to be that case, aligning the abstract words of the Bill of Rights with an understanding of human interdependence that lay deep in African culture.

Drucilla: Karin, I think we should probably bring in your voice here and some of your questions to Justice Sachs.

QUESTION (KARIN): In *The Strange Alchemy of Life and Law*, when you recall the conversations in the ANC that resulted in the idea of the Truth and Reconciliation Commission, you write: "Eventually somebody stood up and asked the simple question: what would my mother say? The figure of 'my mother' represented an ordinary, decent, African working-class woman, not sophisticated but with a good heart and an honest understanding of people and the world — a person whose hard life experiences had promoted a natural sense of honor and integrity" (68).

Commentators have critically engaged with the connection between the TRC and the figure of a woman/a mother, arguing that it had negative implications for women and their own need for reconciliation. It is, for example, common for women to stand in for "nation" in both the colonial and postcolonial setting, making women's bodies the site of actual and metaphorical violence. Women are expected to bear witness silently, to wait and endure patiently, and to thus be redemptive agents in social and political transformation. What is your view on this?

Albie: In 1993, a few months before the first democratic elections, there was a passionate debate in the National Executive of the ANC about what to do about recommendations by a commission set up by the ANC that members of the organization responsible for torture be held accountable. It was one of those debates touching deeply on the morality of the organization that you cannot resolve by a show of hands. Some said torture was torture, whoever committed it, and had to be denounced as being against everything we stood for. Others replied that we had to understand the circumstances of war in Angola in which very young people untrained for security work may well have overstepped the mark. This was the moment when someone — I do not even remember who it was — stood up and said, "What would my mother say?" He told us that his mother would say that there was something unbalanced in our whole approach. Where, she would ask, was the justice in looking at our own faults and not examining the tortures inflicted on us by the rulers of our country?

Kader Asmal then intervened. Kader had given his inaugural lecture at the University of the Western Cape on transitional justice, and the different mechanisms that had been used in different countries to deal with people guilty of atrocious past conduct. Kader now said that what we needed was a Truth Commission that would look across the board at all violations of human rights, as the speaker's mother would have wanted, and not just those of the ANC.

Karin: So there is a separation between two different roles of women, between an imagined woman, as a source of fairness and balance and wisdom that we are attracted to; and the separate role of women being the peace-maker, the conciliator, who will give up sometimes her own just claims for the sake of peace in the family, the community.

Albie: Exactly. It was not the first time that I heard somebody ask: "What would my mother say?" I found that a rather beautiful statement, because the mother was seen as the person who was not ambitious, who was not clever-clever, but who embodied principles of fairness and justice, and expressed things simply and clearly. In fact, looking back, my own mom, a brave and gutsy person, was often very self-deprecating and frequently put herself down in the way you mentioned. This other person was someone quite confident in expressing her sense of justice, her view of what was right or wrong. That was the imagined figure of "my mother."

Karin: So, could you then respond to the second part of my question, even though the specific reference to the mother doesn't link it to the TRC? Even though many women appeared, they were always telling stories about men in their lives, fathers, brothers, husbands, and when they had the special women's hearings, women didn't really want to come out and talk about things personal to them. Someone like Louise du Toit argues that this is very problematic and she's even making this link between our high rape statistics and the lack of reconciliation between the sexes and genders. Mark Sanders (and I actually have another question on Sanders) has argued that commentators have actually missed the very important task that women were performing by telling stories about the dead. I wonder if you could say a bit more, even with Sanders's caveat, about how women were still standing in as the figure of reconciliation during the hearings.

Albie: I have a different viewpoint. In many respects women dominated the proceedings of the TRC. When I shut my eyes and recall the proceedings, my mind fills with images of women testifying. And they were not just testifying for their men folk who were tortured or their sons who lost their hair because of poison. They were testifying for humanity. I found it empowering. I found it strong. Their voice was anti-violence, anti-cruelty. They spoke in their own languages, told their own stories with their own inflexions and nuances. Yet, I also heard that women had great difficulty when speaking about their own experiences as detainees — Zubeida Jaffer told me she didn't want to go to the Truth Commission at all. Ultimately, however, she attended the special session for women, and told her story. But she did not feel she was really telling her story. So maybe you have to speak to her about the deeper question of whether women could speak not as witnesses to the harm done to their men folk, but as protagonists who had themselves been subjected to state abuse.

Let me deviate for a moment. I have spoken about my unabashed support for the right of the oppressed to launch armed action as a component of their struggle against unrelenting oppression. Interestingly, doubts about its wisdom came from two top African leaders for quite different reasons. Albert Luthuli, President of the ANC, was personally reluctant as a devout Christian to give up on the principle of non-violence, though he never spoke out against the armed struggle, and accepted the right of ANC members to join MK. Moses Kotane, General Secretary of the Communist Party, feared that a focus on armed struggle would shift political energy away from mobilizing the black working class to engage in a revolutionary, urban-based insurrection against apartheid. I could add a third unintended consequence. And that is the manner in which the use of armed struggle masculinized the fight for freedom. Though women joined MK as fully participating soldiers, the great bulk of armed combatants were men. Furthermore, the idea of the strong, brave man willing to fight to the death became the prototype of the heroic freedom fighter. In this sense the great gains made by women in the 1950s — the march on the Union Buildings in Pretoria, the organization of women workers in the trade union movement — were overshadowed. Individual women did, of course, exercise the right to be "the strong man." Thenji Mtintso emerged as a formidable commander who carried her feminist ideals with her wherever she went. The story of Phila Ndwandwe, MK combatant who bravely sang the National Anthem before being executed, is apotheosized in the Blue Dress paintings in the Constitutional Court. But mainly it was the men who most directly confronted the forces of apartheid, and men whose deeds and travail as protagonists formed the centerpiece of the testimonies given at the Truth Commission. And their mothers, daughters, sisters, and partners honored them with stories of their courage and pain. *Cantata — Re-wind* in turn pays exquisite musical tribute to the resilience and bravery of the women who testified. By using actual recordings of their evidence, the Cantata ensures, quite literally, that their voices are heard and memorialized.

The Christian confessional dimension of the TRC came partly because its Chair, Desmond Tutu, remained authentic to himself. When presiding he picked up on the meaning of Christianity to the life and death of the poor, allowing their songs and hymns and music to accompany the stories they told in the modest community halls where the TRC met. I personally do not identify with the confessional character of the proceedings. Nor could I participate comfortably in relationships based on the notion of forgiveness — I forgive thee, I forgive thee, I forgive thee. Having grown up in a decidedly secular home, and having shaped my own conscience as a child by refusing to go along with pressure to pretend a belief I did not have, I think I can say that I am profoundly respectful of the importance of every person's conscience and belief. Yet confession and forgiveness are not part of my culture. In my own case, my response to encountering the man who had organized the placing of the bomb in my car was to engage with him on the basis of what I called soft vengeance, not confession. The soft vengeance came from the achievement of the humane ideals for which we had been fighting. The new Constitution and the Truth and Reconciliation Commission were part of this imagined soft vengeance. When Henri — that was his name — bumped into me after he had testified to the TRC, I found myself able to put out my hand to shake his. He went away beaming; I almost fainted. But afterwards he went home and cried for two weeks. I was deeply affected. We had both humanized ourselves, and were beginning to live in the same moral country. Which is what the struggle had been all about.

The Truth Commission had a limited but intense remit — to deal with the torture, assassinations, and other forms of inhuman violence used in the course of political conflict. It has been criticized for focusing on the relatively few security operatives responsible for these crimes, and not on the overall system of apartheid, itself a crime against humanity. Yet apartheid was what the whole democratic transformation, not just a commission, was intended to deal with. The same can be said of the criticism that the Commission failed to investigate sexualized violence, with the consequence, it is said, that rape and sexual molestations continue unabated in our country. Again, this was a dolorous reality that the whole of society had to deal with, not just the Commission.

I do not accept that the Truth Commission in its functioning disempowered and alienated women. It gave women the opportunity to speak about the trauma which they had suffered because of the ill treatment of people close to them; the bodies of their intimate partners and children were rediscovered; they could find out what had happened to the human beings closest to them. I think that intense human relationships of love, affection and closeness and anger, with everything mixed up in the intimacy and effect of people bonded to each other are things that feminism has put on the agenda. I don't think feminism should now undermine the very thing that feminism has brought to the fore.

Karin: Yes, it's a more complex argument that she makes, but ultimately it's about citizenship and she's asking about women's right to citizenship in the new South Africa, questioning whether women enjoy full citizenship. And one of the routes she explores is this aspect of reconciliation.

Albie: I would like to read her full critique. As far as full citizenship and gender are concerned, our Constitution broke important new ground in its definition of freedom.

Because of the intervention of the women's movement, this definition goes well beyond the classical notion of freedom consisting simply of absence of state constraints. The Bill of Rights includes freedom from violence from the state and in private. It also permits freedom to control reproduction. In that sense an element of the feminist notion of freedom was constitutive of citizenship. And there has been legislative follow-up concerning domestic violence and the manner in which charges of sexual violence are heard. Some people say these efforts are puny in terms of impact, but I wouldn't like to undermine even paltry steps in the right direction. I would rather reinforce than dismiss them as unimportant. Categorical lament can be terribly disempowering. Profound analyses of structures of domination in society are important, but they should not prevent us from consolidating and building on small gains that have been made. Having critiqued undue lamentation, however, I'm bound to concede that the situation is indeed lamentable!

QUESTION (DRUCILLA): I wanted to pursue another aspect of the TRC. Antjie Krog and two of her young black colleagues examined the testimony of a woman who was basically dismissed as not being in her right mind. She was the mother of one of the Gugulethu seven. You have always been aware of the connection between learning how to hear others and the significance of spiritual and cultural values of indigenous populations. Again, to refer to this book, the authors emphasize that the testimony of the mother was perfectly coherent in terms of her own cultural metaphors. I think my question to you is related to Karin's in the following sense: how do we actually learn to hear each other? In a certain sense, the point of this book was that that woman could not be heard because she was not speaking the "white" language. In fact, she said she was not going to forgive the murderers of her son. She was not speaking at all in the language of Christian forgiveness, but she was giving to the Commission the experience of an indigenous woman who had suffered a horrific wrong through metaphors that *demanded* that we be able to hear an African spirituality, and yet somehow or another that mutual hearing process faltered. You know it is a very careful book, it does not reach any giant conclusions but it is certainly an important reminder that we need to be able, not only to hear women, but particularly we need to recognize that many black women speak an entirely a different language.

Albie: That was one of the themes of the play *Lost in Translation*. To the extent that the process brought these issues to the fore, they became part of the national dialogue. Speaking about the Gugulethu Seven, though, you are probably familiar with the film *Long Night's Journey into Day*. It ends with the mothers of the Seven confronting the African policeman, from their community, who had participated in the assassinations. When they started shouting at him — I knew how it would end, not because I understood any motive the film-makers might have had, but because I could understand the trajectory people who had to speak and denounce and express their anger before they could reach the question of reconciliation. You don't start with forgiveness, you end with forgiveness. There he was with his head bowed, and one after the other the mothers were castigating him and shouting at him. It was important that he bowed his head: it meant that he acknowledged the moral wrongness of what he had done. Only after he had done that, could they embrace him. It was intensely moving for me. The scene showed Africans drawing on their culture to find their own way to forgiveness. It was important for the women. They didn't want to live with perpetual fury deep inside themselves, especially if it targeted someone who would continue to be their neighbor. Their sons in that sense had not died in vain, but had been part of a struggle for a better world. These women wanted to find a way of living with this man whose actions had cruelly affected them. It was a form of uBuntu, if you like, of transcendence of rage and bitterness. But it was not a smily-smily uBuntu (let's all be brothers and sisters together, and forget the past). It was a painful uBuntu. He had to listen to them and hear them and acknowledge their pain. In that sense he could become an honest person through bearing the weight of his wrongdoing, as expressed through the mouths of the mothers he had injured so grievously.

QUESTION (KARIN): One more question on uBuntu: Sanders, in another work, *Ambiguities of Witnessing*, describes uBuntu as an ethics that "continually marks and remarks a loss of humanity, and of human dignity" and argues that it will never accept final restoration because it "resides in a perpetual remarking of default" (120). How can this understanding of uBuntu support uBuntu as a critical response to traditional accounts of law and constitutionalism?

Albie: I think uBuntu can manifest itself in circumstances of success as well as of distress. Sanders takes note of it in the context of its capacity to deal with the dire. The Truth Commission concerned itself with violation, stress, and disrepair. I am not familiar with his work, but learn a lot from the focus and tone of the extract you have shown me. uBuntu is undoubtedly evoked by hurt and disrepair. But it does not function simply as a sort of fire engine that puts out moral fires wherever they occur. I agree with Sanders's notion of the eternal necessity to restore violated relationships. Society is always undergoing evolution and change. I don't believe in inherent sin, but I do believe in intrinsic contradiction. Life is contradiction, contradiction is life. There are no fixed horizons of accomplishment, as if somehow a constitutional paradise could be reached, if only . . . Constitutions are not based on living the ideal life, but on using principles of the ideal to deal with and ameliorate the imperfections and corruptions of the actual world we live in. I think in a way that gives something of an answer to Sanders. Maybe I'm misreading him, I haven't read his . . . was it an article or a book?

Karin: It's a book, yes. I think Drucilla also thought it linked to what you said about the women, so it's underscored the painful uBuntu. I think quite often critics against uBuntu would say that it is over-romanticized, over-idealized, I think the uBuntu project has done enough to counter that, but what I think is important here is also uBuntu as critique. So uBuntu can do difficult work. I think white people often use uBuntu in a very wrong way because they don't want to give up certain things. uBuntu does demand that we treat one another in a human way, and as you put it, Albie, this demand can

cause distress. What Sanders is saying is that uBuntu has a critical cut, and I think that side of uBuntu should be explored more in difficult times.

Albie: Yes, it is affirmative and it is demanding. It is very close to the idea of fraternity (which can be objectionable as a sexist term). At its core, it is human solidarity, human interdependence. In some ways it is a very revolutionary notion. It is not based on forms of conquest of power in the way that we used to envision revolution, as a statist attempt to reconfigure society to emancipate everybody. It is a much more participatory notion, a pluralistic and empowering notion, compelling people to advance their lives and influence public life in neighborhoods, communities, different forms of organizations, faith communities, and groups like that.

I adhere to uBuntu not because it's an African term or because it has a feel-good quality. I encountered it when I was practicing as an advocate at the Bar in Cape Town. The people from the townships, called "locations" then, would get together in my office, and would discuss things amongst themselves and discuss, and discuss, and discuss to get the fairest outcome in the most difficult of situations. I was affected by the deep human solidarity amongst poor people helping other poor people. We did not use the word uBuntu then. But poor people would share what little bit that they had, while those who had made a bit of money would be much more self-centered and much more individualistic.

Years later I was influenced by Oliver Tambo's philosophy. And when I did research on capital punishment as part of my doctoral studies, I was thrilled to discover that many of the greatest traditional leaders had been opposed to capital punishment, stating that blood should not follow blood. I've been criticized by Johan van der Walt for my concurring opinion in *Makwanyane*, the capital punishment case. In his eloquent way he accused me of plucking out what I wanted to see in traditional African culture. Not so, Johan. But I have lived with the solidarity of the struggle itself. I've taken part in the debate and discussions. It is a very real and live principle, uBuntu, not just a nice romantic notion to be painted on as a balm to calm things down when there's stress.

Sadly, the very failure of so many white people to accept the degree to which they were advantaged in the past, to acknowledge the extent to which and continue to enjoy unjust advantages today, locks them into denial of the depth of African values. Often people see uBuntu as saying, "Okay, it's all over, thank you brothers and sisters for being so forgiving, everything's fine, let's forget the past and all move forward together, long live uBuntu." They are completely mistaken about the complexity and the psychological and philosophical richness of uBuntu, of the human solidarity it connotes between people, often in desperate circumstances, tenaciously looking after each other in such a strong, generous, and healthy way.

So looking back, I see the idea of an epic storming of heaven by historically chosen cadres of progress, giving way to a more universalistic notion of the meek, the kind, the giving, inheriting the earth. Yet what we've lost in heroism, we have gained in humanity. uBuntu pays tribute to the tenacity of intimate sharing and the richness of mutual involvement. Its focus, then, is less on the grand structures of society and more on the subtle textures and nuanced character of mundane interactions. By its nature, the law mediates between the structures, the culture, and the detail of daily life. But this emancipatory impulse and humane vision must always be there.

Drucilla: I find it interesting that you connect uBuntu with fraternity. I think one of the aspects of uBuntu that gets missed by the critics of uBuntu is precisely the critical edge which must be there if we are going to develop relations of mutuality as human beings who are given equal respect. I remember when I was working with a Sangoma. A young man stole a TV. A young man who was orphaned at a young age. The Sangoma felt he was outside the community, and the most important thing was to bring him back into the community. When he stole the TV, she did not turn him over to the police. He had to take the TV back to the man. Nor was the man expected to forgive. She then told the young boy that he now had an obligation to this man to work for him for the next six months. He was to take care of his needs, and in the course of so doing, he would learn uBuntu. This example shows how complex the demands of uBuntu are. The young man's inclusion in the community demanded a deep re-engagement with the person he had wronged. Now of course many whites are uncomfortable with the story when I tell it, because he was ordered and as you know, very few people disobey a Sangoma, although she has no police force behind her. So he was ordered to work for the man. But in the course of it, what happened was he became included into the community. In fact, he ended up living with the man until he graduated from high school. So it's that understanding that what is lost, isn't just between this individual who lost a TV and the one who stole it, it's the entire community is hurt if we don't bring those who are excluded into it, into this kind of engagement with one and other.

Albie: This reminds me of a powerful experience I had not long after arriving in Mozambique. They did not have prisons in the rural areas. Community service was the only way that they could "punish" people. The whole of their justice system was based on reintegration into society. What Samora Machel insisted on was that community service must be useful in itself. To get people to dig holes and fill them up again destroyed the dignity of labor. To get people to build a bus shelter or to plant flowers, on the other hand, actually worked because it tapped into a deep cultural resource, community interdependence.

For more serious offenders there was a large open prison farm near Maputo. I could never find it because it had no walls, and I would drive past, and drive back and look for the prisoner in charge. The prisoners worked on an honor system — the penalty for absconding or other violation of the rules was to be sent to a real prison with bars. I was amused one day to find why the normally calm prisoner in charge was beside himself. Serving a 10-year sentence because he had stolen a large sum of money from the government, he was now in a fury about the local population who would simply walk on to the prisoners' fields at night and steal the maize growing there. "No respect for other people's property!" he thundered. Sadly, the civil wars in Mozambique destroyed all these humane and creative endeavors. But it was evident that the principles of uBuntu and restorative justice had huge cultural resonance there, just as I was sure they had that, given the opportunity to flourish, they would have in South Africa.

And it is pleasing to see that today the underlying notions of uBuntu have been incorporated into child law in South Africa, and that the courts are exploring ways of humanizing and strengthening aspects of criminal and civil law more generally by infusions of restorative justice.

I have fought since I was a child for the right to make my own decisions, in keeping with my own conscience. I'm a great believer in personal autonomy, coupled with personal responsibility. But I have also learned that living in community with others, sharing hopes and ideals, learning to give and receive, has been enormously enriching for me. The miracle of South Africa was not produced by the wonderful Mandela (though he was wonderful) or the wise De Klerk (though he showed wisdom). It flowed from the confluence of uBuntu, human rights ideas, and political dialogue. In that sense, uBuntu is not a gracious add-on, it is inscribed in the very sinews of all that is best in our new constitutional order.

QUESTION (DRUCILLA): You have distinguished between discovery, justification, and persuasion in the actual process of judging, and indeed relied on a reading of Immanuel Kant to discuss how the process of judging demands an enlarged mentality. Although I disagreed with Jennifer Nedelsky's reading of Immanuel Kant, I think that Kant's notion of the *sensus communis*, as long as it is understood as a should-be of a community that is brought into being in the act of judging and not as an actual community, is helpful in understanding your own view of judgment. In your most recent book, *The Strange Alchemy of Life and Law*, you write about how a judge judges. You underscore the role of emotion and discovery and imagination in trying to envision how the ideals of the Bill of Rights are to be developed. This role of judgment completely runs against the grain of black letter lawyers who insist

either that law is based on the plain letter interpretation of language, or upon rigid rules of interpretation. Could you say more about your own view of judgment as it actually was developed in the course of your work on the Bench?

Albie: I wasn't trying to base myself on philosophical principles and apply them to judging. On the contrary, I tried to describe something I was actually experiencing. The big issue for me was: why was it so hard to write a judgment (opinion)? When you read published judgments they seem to flow with a sense of pure logic and rightness. But if the process of producing judgments was so rational and straightforward, how could colleagues, whom I admired enormously, disagree with each other? And how could I dissent from them? To confound my belief in pure reasoning even more, in my first years as a judge, when I happened to be a bath person, an answer to a legal question I had long been battling with and unable to resolve arose unbidden into my head often clothed in completely formed and eloquent words, as I lay inert and unthinking in the bathtub. This, too, worried me. Judging was supposed to be one of the most objective, rational, and thought-through of all human activities. Yet here were key ideas usually relating to fundamental organizing principles, popping effortlessly and without conscious reasoning, into my mind. What was going on, I wondered. And why was it, if the logic of a decision was so simple, I would write as many as 20 different drafts of a single judgment. This huffing and puffing to get the right answer went against the logic of logic. Why was it so difficult to get it all right? I should stress that my quest at that stage was not to find a philosophical underpinning to give more coherence to my judicial reasoning. It was to describe as a participant observer the actual process of decision-making. In particular, it was to convey something of how turbulent, rather than precise and rational, the process of judicial reasoning actually was.

The answer was given to me not in a bath, but over a dinner table one night, by a University of Toronto political scientist, not a lawyer. He told me of the difference between the logic of reason and the logic of discovery. And so, through him, I discovered discovery. And having discovered it, suddenly it was everywhere.

After reading my manuscript, Justice Ruth Bader Ginsberg of the US Supreme Court kindly pointed me to the book *Blink* by Malcolm Gladwell in America. It dealt with the sudden moments in which many important decisions were made. And a psychologist friend told me of the three Bs: bed, bus, and bath, in which many discoveries were made. Yet I hadn't seen anything in legal literature on discovery of organizing principles. You could discover a document or a witness of even a precedent, but not an idea. Antony Akerman had described constitutional moments when qualitative changes had taken place in judicial reasoning that couldn't be ascribed simply to the evolution of precedent. But I was concerned with something far less grandiose than profound constitutional moments for society. I wanted to discern and describe a process far more personal to myself, a sudden intuitive leap in my own understanding of a legal problem. A mass of inchoate material goes around in my head, the more I read, the more confusing it gets, and the more I hear argument, the more I battle to get through the thicket of possibilities. Then apparently from nowhere, there is a moment of illumination, a key understanding that connects up themes and ideas, and allows all the dissonant details to settle into place. The dialectic is resolved, and I can move forward. I wanted to bring out the reality of that experience, and in so doing move away from the notion that judges function as though on rationality autopilot.

One of the few things you can be sure about as far as judicial truth is concerned is that it is not self-evident. This is why the Kantian distinction between reasoning and judgment, referred to in your question, becomes so relevant. I accept your proposition that Immanuel Kant had in mind an imagined community, and not a sociological one, that would establish the markers for the judging process. In my own case, I would in practice intuitively construct an imagined, Weberian ideal type of a legal community. I would semi-consciously construct a mental model of core features extracted from my awareness of the sprawling, contradictory, and very active thing we called the legal world. Yet, whether the legal community was the actual one or a purely imagined one, or something of both, the judging process inevitably went beyond pure logic and engaged with questions of weighing and values. And this is where the element that US Supreme Court Justice Brennan called passion, would fairly and squarely come into the picture. In his view — one which I share — constitutional adjudication involves a comingling of reason and passion. He deliberately chose the word "passion" because it appeared to be the direct opposite of reason. But in this context, passion does not connote anything as exciting as wild sexual abandon, but only intense human empathy. It is the warm beating heart that battles with the cold, rigorous mind, that produces what Brennan regarded as good adjudication. What this adds up to is a going-beyond the notion of the judge as a machine-like instrument of pure reason, arriving at her or his decisions purely on the basis of established evidence and logical analysis, without any regard to questions of intensity, context, and impact.

I must stress that the only experience I have had as a judge has been on the Constitutional Court. This Court hears constitutional matters, and, in general, only responds to applications that have a reasonable prospect of success. By its nature, the Court prowls around the frontiers of constitutionalism, specializing in borderline cases that could go either way. It might be that most judicial work in most courts is based on evidence and reasoning where no new conceptual discoveries are made, the values involved all point in the same direction, the appropriate weighting to be given to the relevant elements is quite clear, and the judicial heart and judicial mind can lie down peacefully with each other. But in borderline cases of great moment, there will be an intrinsic turbulence in the judging process that cannot be stilled simply by the application of pure logic. What fascinated me at case conferences was how my colleagues, each coming up with impeccable logic, would arrive at totally different conclusions. Clearly, something more than pure reasoning was involved. It was that "something more" that I sought to locate and describe.

I am not sure that all of my colleagues are enthusiastic about the manner in which I describe the process of judicial decision-making. I suspect they feel that it imports too much subjectivity, and underplays the degree of detachment that a good judge is obliged to bring to bear, whatever her or his personal feelings on a matter might be. Yet my purpose has not been to promote a theory of the judicial function, or to advance a philosophical foundation for developing principled approaches to constitutional reasoning. It has been, rather, to introspect on and record the way we have actually been functioning. This involves candid acknowledgement of the principled disciplining of the elements of subjectivity that I believe inevitably and appropriately enter into modern constitutional adjudication. Judges are not moralists at large, armed with a constitutional text the words of which they can interpret as they like. While grammar, classification, and definitional reasoning play an important role, much of their work today involves weighing and balancing; applying broad values to narrow situations; reconciling and harmonizing values that overlap, compete, and collide in the same factual setting; and utilizing principles of proportionality to come to a conclusion. More and more, their work moves away from a concern with determining the frontiers between right and wrong, and increasingly in a modern pluralist society, it focuses on holding the balance between right and right.

There are two observations on the nature of our new constitutional dispensation in South Africa that are frequently quoted, but rarely brought together. The first is that the Constitution is transformative rather than preservative [Karl Klare]. The second is that it requires us to move from a culture of authority to one of justification [Etienne Mureinik]. I believe these ideas are intrinsically conjoined, consequences for the judicial function, in the open and democratic society envisaged in the Constitution. In the first place, though judges must be impartial in terms of giving a dispassionate hearing to all parties, they should not be neutral in relation to laws and practices that go against the deep morality firmly implanted in the text of the Constitution. If judges are to honor their oath to do justice to all under the Constitution and the law, they will take definite sides on questions over which others in the community may be divided: racism, sexism, homophobia, disability rights, and xenophobia; torture and the right to a fair trial; and the state's duty to provide reasonable access to housing, health, education, food, and water. Furthermore, the judiciary is bound to acknowledge historic and continuing structures of disadvantage, to place the values of human dignity, equality, and freedom at the forefront of their reasoning, and to draw what sustenance they can from international law and foreign judicial pronouncements. And in affirming the new culture of justification, the courts must not only require the legislature to justify the manner in which it is meeting its constitutional obligations. The judges must justify their own decisions. In my view, this requires them to come up with judgments that are persuasive and accessible, firmly anchored in constitutional principle, rooted in the social, cultural, and economic realities of the country, and imbued with the values which inform the Constitution. Principled and transparent judging in this context cannot rely solely on logical drill. The manner in which the values operate, the weighting that is done, the balancing effected, and the proportionality or otherwise that is determined, need to be spelt out, and as candidly and persuasively as possible.

QUESTION (KARIN): You've previously recalled that you knew Afrikaans author, Uys Krige, and that he played a significant role in your youth and your own development. Would you like to elaborate and maybe say something about the relation between law and literature, or a legal/literary engagement?

Albie: When in the struggle days I wrote a paper for the ANC on culture, people said, "Albie, why are you bringing culture into politics?" When, more recently, I got involved with the vision of the design of the Constitutional Court, it was, "Albie, what motivates you to bring art into the realm of judging?" In fact, it was the other way round — it was culture that brought me into politics, and culture that accompanied me onto the Bench.

It would have been in the early 1950s, I'm 16 and my mother says that Uys Krige, in whose basement flat we had once stayed, is giving a series of lectures I might be interested in. So out of curiosity, knowing that he was a poet, and I liked poetry, I went.

The first poet he spoke about was Federico Lorca, a Spanish poet. I did not know they even had poets in Spain. I knew they had bull fights and funny food, not people like Shakespeare and Shelley. For maybe three hours, Uys walked up and down on the platform, talking non-stop to us in English, Afrikaans, Spanish, and bit of French. It was phenomenal, both the delivery and the content. And what was hugely important for me was how he linked poetry, which was soulful, personal, and intimate, with the big public events of the world. The next week he spoke on the Chilean poet, Pablo Neruda. Poets in Latin America, where they had alligators, rather than crocodiles, and the Amazon which was shorter than the Nile, and people said mañana and danced the tango? Yet, instead of listening to a self-conscious analysis of the rhyming schemes and use of metaphor by Wordsworth and Keats, I was treated to three more glorious hours of poetry, about love, the revolution, and the human soul. Two weeks later, I joined the Modern Youth Society, and 10 months later I was leading a group of four young white people who joined the Defiance of Unjust Laws Campaign by sitting on a seat marked Non-Whites Only.

I hope people will never stop calling me an idealist and a romantic. Idealism and poetry do not stop me from seeing the injustice of the world. On the contrary, they sharpen my awareness of pain, unfairness, and injustice, and intensify my eagerness to see change. They lead me to yearn for the positive, and to look for the humanity even in your enemies, without condoning what they are doing.

And when on the Bench, I could never separate out the legal and the literary. Once, just once, I went out of my way to write a boring, purely technical judgment, just to prove to my colleagues that if I really set my mind to it, I could write a judgment that had no vivacity and no resonance, just enough to resolve a particular dispute without raising any question at all of the significance of the law for those affected by it.

For the rest, the words of my judgment come out as they come out. As I see them, rights by their very nature embody more than interests. They incorporate pain, imagination, history, and hope. Their bearers are human beings possessed of intelligence and sensibility. If I am compelled to squeeze all vivacity and resonance out of my judgments, then what I write will not truly convey the thought processes that led to the outcome. Just as reason and passion inter-penetrate, so words and ideals have a complex interrelationship. And if I don't tell the story the way my conscience feels and understands the trajectory of my thought, then I am not living up to my responsibility as a judge. Our oath requires us not merely to resolve disputes, but to do justice to all. And true justice, I believe, wears its garments with dignity and pride.

QUESTION (DRUCILLA): I want to come back to the connection between what you just said about your engagement with poetry as a way of bringing you to politics through seeing things that you couldn't see before. Through poetry, we are able to hear and see realities that are completely foreign to us. A crucial aspect of poetry is to open the space for the unseen to be imagined and the unheard to be heard. Art seeks the impossible in that it often strives to envision what has fallen into invisibility. What do you see as the connection between poetry and art more broadly speaking, and the nation-building project you've described earlier?

Albie: I have a short, sweet, and, I hope, convincing answer to this question. But before giving it, allow me to refer to the special role the Bill of Rights played in fostering what you refer to as nation-building.

The whole project of negotiating our Constitution was extraordinary. It was not easy. There were serious breakdowns. Discussions lasted well into the night. We rarely slept. We were exhausted. But we kept arguing, disputing, debating, at times getting quite angry with each other. The outcome was amazing and wonderful. But it was not a miracle. Miracles are not made out of meetings with Minutes, Matters Arising, and Any Other Business. Endless discussions and debates are not the stuff of miracles. It was really our intelligence, sense of history, and commitment that saw us through. Oliver Tambo had succumbed to a stroke, but his vision of the role of the Bill of Rights proved to be central. Looking back, I can see how crucial it was not only in establishing the framework for a non-racial and non-sexist society, and not only in ensuring that hard-won freedoms would not easily be frittered away. The Bill of Rights has become the cornerstone of what you refer to as nation-building. I use the term nation-building with some hesitation, because it may hint at state-driven loyalty oaths and patriotic parades. I prefer the idea of the nation growing organically on the basis of equal citizenship and a shared commitment to certain basic rights. Whatever the phraseology used, however, I am convinced that the Bill of Rights, placed right at the beginning of the Constitution, has been foundational to the achievement of the notion of unity in diversity, which in turn is central to the growth of shared loyalty and identification with the nation.

And the short answer to your question is as follows: our jazz musicians wrote our Constitution in music long before we lawyers wrote it in words.

Drucilla: Thank you so much Justice Sachs.
Karin: Yes, thank you very much.

Albie Sachs with his son Oliver Sachs, photo by Steve Gordon

Source: Albie Sachs documentary collection at the Mayibuye Centre.

Notes

Introduction

1 A. Sachs, *The Strange Alchemy of Life and Law* (Oxford and New York: Oxford University Press, 2009), p. 1.
2 See also A. Hutchinson, *Laughing at the Gods: Great Judges and How They Made the Common Law* (Cambridge: Cambridge University Press, 2012), in which he reflects on the work of amongst others Mansfield, Marshall, Holmes, and also Sachs.
3 See, e.g. M. Mamdani, "When does reconciliation turn into a denial of justice?" in S. Nolutshungu (ed.), *Memorial Lectures* (Pretoria: Human and Scientific Research Council, 1998).
4 See, e.g. M. Ramphele, *Laying Ghosts to Rest. Dilemmas of the Transformation in South Africa* (Cape Town: NB Publishers, 2008); and N. Alexander, *An Ordinary Country: Issues in the Transition from Apartheid to Democracy in South Africa* (Pietermaritzburg: University of Natal Press, 2003).
5 See, e.g. F. V. Z. Slabbert, *The Other Side of History. An Anecdotal Reflection on Political Transition in South Africa* (Johannesburg and Cape Town: Jonathan Ball Publishers, 2006).
6 N. Ndebele, "The rediscovery of the ordinary" (1986) 12 *Journal of South African Studies* 143; and Mamdani, "When does reconciliation turn into a denial of justice?", above n. 3.
7 S. Biko, *I Write What I Like* (Johannesburg: Picador Africa, 2004). See also X. Mangcu, *Biko. A Biography* (Cape Town: Tafelberg, 2012).
8 K. Ross, *A Concise History of South Africa* (Cambridge: Cambridge University Press, 2008); and L. Thompson, *A History of South Africa* (2001).
9 R. Spitz and M. Chaskalson, *The Politics of Transition: A Hidden History of South Africa's Negotiated Settlement* (Oxford: Hart, 2000).
10 L. Ackermann, "The legal nature of the South African constitutional revolution" (2004) *New Zealand Law Review* 4: 633; and L. Ackermann, *Human Dignity: Lodestar for Equality in South Africa* (Cape Town: Juta Law Books, 2012).
11 H. Kelsen, *Pure Theory of Law* (Berkeley, CA: University of California Press, 1967); and H. Kelsen, *Peace through Law* (Union, NJ: The Lawbook Exchange, 2000).
12 Preamble to the Constitution of the Republic of South Africa as adopted on May 8, 1996 and amended on October 11, 1996 by the Constitutional Assembly.
13 See ss. 25 (right to equitable access to land and to security of tenure); 26 (right to have access to adequate housing and not to be evicted arbitrarily); 27 (rights to have access to health care services, water, food, and social assistance, and the right not to be refused emergency medical treatment); and 29 (right to have access to basic and further education).

14 The same powers of interpretation, determination of disputes, and remedy that courts have with respect to civil rights, they also have with respect to socio-economic rights.
15 A. Sachs, *Protecting Human Rights in a New South Africa* (Contemporary South African Debates) (Cape Town: Oxford University Press, 1991); and *Advancing Human Rights in South Africa* (Contemporary South African Debates) (Cape Town: Oxford University Press, 1993).
16 See s. 24.
17 See, e.g. s. 15 of the Constitution protecting freedom of religion, belief, and opinion; s. 30 protecting language and culture; and s. 31 protecting cultural, religious, and linguistic communities.
18 Section 9, which, apart from a guarantee of equality before the law and a prohibition on unfair discrimination, explicitly provides that legislative and other measures must be designed to ensure substantive equality.
19 See s. 8, which declares all organs of state as well as all private parties ("natural and juristic persons") bound by the rights in the Constitution's Bill of Rights.
20 For two recent overviews of these debates and progressive engagements with the issues raised in it, see: A. J. Van der Walt, *Property and Constitution* (Pretoria: Pretoria University Law Press, 2012); and D. M. Davis and K. Klare, "Transformative constitutionalism and the common and customary law" (2010) *South African Journal on Human Rights* 26: 403.
21 Sachs, *The Strange Alchemy of Life and Law*, above n. 1, p. 27.
22 Kelsen, *Pure Theory of Law*, above n. 11.
23 Sachs, *The Strange Alchemy of Life and Law*, above n. 1.
24 See, e.g. T. Terreblanche, *The History of Inequality in South Africa 1652–2002* (Pietermaritzburg: University of Natal Press, 2002); and T. Terreblanche, *Lost in Transformation* (Johannesburg: KMM Review Publishing Co., 2012).
25 M. Mbeki, *Architects of Poverty: Why African Capitalism Needs Changing* (Johannesburg: Pan Macmillan, 2009); P. Bond, H. Chitonge, and A. Hoffman (eds.), *The Accumulation of Capital in Southern Africa: Rosa Luxemburg's Contemporary Relevance* (Berlin and Durban: Rosa Luxemburg Foundation and Centre for Civil Society, 2007).
26 F. Fukuyama, *The End of History and the Last Man* (New York: Free Press, 1992).
27 *Port-Elizabeth Municipality* v. *Various Occupiers* 2005 (1) SA 217 (CC), para. 18.

Chapter 1

1 É. Balibar, *Politics and the Other Scene*, trans. C. Jones, J. Swenson, and C. Turner (London and New York: Verso, 2002). Balibar has elaborated the notion of civility further in *Violence et civilité* (Paris: Galilée, 2010), English translation forthcoming from Columbia University Press.
2 See C. O'Regan, "From form to substance: the constitutional jurisprudence of Laurie Ackermann," and D. Cornell, "Bridging the span toward justice: Laurie Ackermann and the ongoing architectonic of dignity jurisprudence" in A. J. Barnard-Naudé, D. Cornell, and F. du Bois (eds.), *Dignity, Freedom and the Post-Apartheid Legal Order: The Critical Jurisprudence of Laurie Ackermann* (Cape Town: Juta, 2008), pp. 1–17 and 18–46.
3 For an excellent discussion of Kelsen's notion of revolution and the meaning of the South African substantive revolution, see L. Ackermann, "The legal nature of the South African constitutional revolution" (2004) *New Zealand Law Review* 633: 678–9.
4 I am well aware of the searing critiques of the transition as an "elite transition"; see Patrick Bond's compelling argument in *Elite Transition: From Apartheid to Neoliberalism in South Africa* (London and Ann Arbor, MI: Pluto Press; and Pietermaritzburg: University of Natal Press, 2000). I would certainly agree with Bond that the ANC

has capitulated to neoliberal capitalism as an inevitability, and that this puts severe limits on what the Constitutional Court can do in the name of achieving a just society in the new South Africa. Exactly what those limits are would take us back to Marx's critique of Hegel, and this is part of a larger project that I am working on now. I do want to note, however, that Steven L. Robins has rightfully pointed out that Bond's analysis may be too one-sided, in that the mass movements of South Africa continue to take the idea of a socialist revolution seriously, and often appeal to the new constitutional rights as a way to demand entitlement and mark the failures of the reigning economic policies. See S. L. Robins, *From Revolution to Rights in South Africa: Social Movements, NGOs and Popular Politics after Apartheid* (Pietermaritzburg: University of Kwazulu-Natal Press, 2008).

5 See again: Robins, *From Revolution to Rights in South Africa*, above n. 4.

6 É. Balibar, *Masses, Classes, Ideas: Studies on Politics and Philosophy before and after Marx*, trans. J. Swenson (London and New York: Routledge, 1994), pp. 46–7. See also É. Balibar, *La proposition de l'égaliberté* (Paris: Presses Universitaires de France, 2010).

7 The Constitution of the Republic of South Africa, Act 108 of 1996.

8 A. Sachs, *The Strange Alchemy of Life and Law* (Oxford: Oxford University Press, 2009).

9 Sachs, *The Strange Alchemy of Life and Law*, above n. 8, p. 10.

10 Sachs, *The Strange Alchemy of Life and Law*, above n. 8, p. 13.

11 Sachs, *The Strange Alchemy of Life and Law*, above n. 8, p. 15.

12 Sachs, *The Strange Alchemy of Life and Law*, above n. 8, pp. 16–17.

13 Sachs, *The Strange Alchemy of Life and Law*, above n. 8, pp. 20–1.

14 Sachs, *The Strange Alchemy of Life and Law*, above n. 8, pp. 21–2.

15 Balibar, *Politics and the Other Scene*, above n. 1, pp. 29–30.

16 É. Balibar, *We, the People of Europe? Reflections on Transnational Citizenship* (Princeton, NJ: Princeton University Press, 2004), p. 131.

17 Balibar, *Politics and the Other Scene*, above n. 1, pp. 30–1.

18 "In my opinion, the approach that our Constitution required us to adopt was neither a purely libertarian one, nor simply communitarian. It was dignitarian. Respect for human dignity united the right to be autonomous with the need to recognize that we all live in communities. It was the fundamental right of all human beings to have their basic human dignity respected, that linked the right to freedom with the right to bread" (Sachs, *The Strange Alchemy of Life and Law*, above n. 8, p. 173).

19 Sachs, *The Strange Alchemy of Life and Law*, above n. 8, p. 87.

20 See, for instance, M. Sanders, *Ambiguities of Witnessing: Law and Literature in the Time of a Truth Commission* (Stanford, CA: Stanford University Press, 2007). See also K. van Marle, "Laughter, refusal, friendship — thoughts on a 'jurisprudence of generosity'" in K. van Marle (ed.), *Refusal, Transition and Post-Apartheid Law* (Stellenbosch: African Sun MeDIA, 2009), pp. 15–28. Of course, these are only two of the many critiques of the TRC. Mahmood Mamdani famously argued that the entire structure of the TRC was flawed, and that it focused on victims and perpetrators as opposed to the much broader category of beneficiaries, and as a result undermined the necessary call for massive reparative measures to be taken in the name of justice (M. Mamdani, "Amnesty or impunity? A preliminary critique of the report of the Truth and Reconciliation Commission of South Africa (TRC)" (2002) *Diacritics* 32: 33–59). Indeed, Mamdani and Sampie Terreblanche called for a Justice and Reconciliation Commission in 1997. In 2008, Mamdani, Terreblanche, and this author called again for the creation of a Justice and Reconciliation Commission, given the dire economic reality of the new South Africa under conditions of neoliberal capitalism.

21 Sachs, *The Strange Alchemy of Life and Law*, above n. 8, p. 157.

22 Sachs, *The Strange Alchemy of Life and Law*, above n. 8, pp. 214–15.

23 I have written about uBuntu and the *Makwanyane* decision in my "Remarks for the roundtable in honor of Justice Yvonne Mokgoro" (paper presented at the conference on "The Future of the uBuntu Project," Pretoria, South Africa, August 19–20, 2010).
24 Balibar, *Politics and the Other Scene*, above n. 1, p. 25.
25 Sachs, *The Strange Alchemy of Life and Law*, above n. 8, p. 41.
26 Sachs, *The Strange Alchemy of Life and Law*, above n. 8, pp. 45–6.
27 Cf. my "Remarks for the roundtable in honor of Justice Yvonne Mokgoro."
28 The author debated with Albie Sachs in 2004 as to whether or not uBuntu could be a justiciable constitutional principle. At that time, he argued against such a deployment of uBuntu, but has later changed his mind and has become one of the leading jurisprudential voices on the meaning of uBuntu. See D. Cornell, "A call for a nuanced jurisprudence: uBuntu, dignity and reconciliation" in D. Cornell and N. Muvangua (eds.), *uBuntu and the Law: African Ideals and Postapartheid Jurisprudence* (New York: Fordham University Press, 2011), pp. 369–79.
29 M. More, "South Africa under and after apartheid" in K. Wiredu (ed.), *A Companion to African Philosophy* (Oxford: Blackwell, 2006), pp. 149 and 156–7.
30 See the discussion of uBuntu-botho as it is used to strike down the use of primogeniture and gender inequality in the first Bhe case, in Cornell and Muvangua (eds.), *uBuntu and the Law*, above n. 28, pp. 257–68.
31 Sachs, *The Strange Alchemy of Life and Law*, above n. 8, pp. 154–5.
32 I have throughout relied on the theoretical work of Étienne Balibar to help us understand the complex dilemmas and their solutions that are presented by the South African Constitution that has taken the institutionalization of equaliberty so seriously. We have also seen how Justice Sachs at least brings civility into the realm of equaliberty, and indeed, as one way of thinking about a judicial solution to the aporias of competing rights situations. Although Balibar always recognizes that it is Hegel, in his notion of the *Rechtsstaat*, that gives us the primary philosophical justification of the institutionalization of civility, Balibar himself always questions to what degree civility, or perhaps a more wide-ranging notion such as uBuntu-botho can actually be institutionalized. To quote Balibar: "Disincorporation is a double-edged sword. The political hypothesis of a civility 'from below' cannot, then, choose between the strategy (or language) of the becoming-majoritarian or the becoming-minoritarian of resistance, since it defines itself both as an alternative to the violence inherent in the state, and as a remedy for the state's impotence in respect of the two faces of cruelty. If this is not a theoretical choice, then it is a conjunctural question, a question of the art of politics — and perhaps simply of art, since the only means civility has at its disposal are statements, signs and roles" (Balibar, *Politics and the Other Scene*, above n. 1, p. 35). Returning to the title of this chapter, "Comrade judge," we are left with what may well be the difference between being a judge and being a philosopher, at least to some degree. But Justice Sachs has always been concerned with the institutionalization of civility, even in the context of the armed struggle, so it is interesting to at least conjecture — and certainly Justice Sachs indicates this strongly in his judicial autobiography — that the institutionalization of civility has informed the policies of the ANC long before the formation of the Constitution.
33 *Dikoko* v. *Mokhatla* 2006 (6) SA 235 (cc).
34 *Dikoko* v. *Mokhatla* 2006 (6) SA 235 (cc).
35 I have tried to argue that Marxists do not need to reject rights or constitutionalism, while taking very seriously this heritage of deep suspicion about rights talks, in D. Cornell, "Should a Marxist believe in rights?" (1984) *Praxis International* 1: 45–56.
36 Sachs, *The Strange Alchemy of Life and Law*, above n. 8, pp. 171–2.
37 Sachs, *The Strange Alchemy of Life and Law*, above n. 8, p. 177.

38 Sachs, *The Strange Alchemy of Life and Law*, above n. 8, p. 179.
39 I want to thank Jane Gordon for her insight into the significance of this change of narration.
40 Balibar, *Masses, Classes, Ideas*, above n. 6, p. 221.
41 *Port-Elizabeth Municipality* v. *Various Occupiers* 2005 (1) SA 217 (CC), para. 23.
42 *Port Elizabeth*, para. 32.
43 *Port Elizabeth*, para. 37.
44 H. Arendt, *The Origins of Totalitarianism* (New York: Harcourt, 1976), p. 298.
45 *Residents of Joe Slovo Community, Western Cape* v. *Thubelisha Homes and Others* (CCT 22/08) [2009] ZACC 16; 2009 (9) BCLR 847 (CC); 2010 (3) SA 454 (CC) (June 10, 2009).
46 Residents of Joe Slovo Community.
47 Professor Sampie Terreblanche, the author of *History of Inequality in South Africa* (Pietermaritzburg: University of Kwazulu-Natal Press, 2003), raised this question to Justice Sachs, when Sachs presented an uBuntu workshop at the University of Cape Town in 2009.
48 See also the following contributions to *The Accumulation of Capital in Southern Africa: Rosa Luxemburg Political Education Seminar 2006* (Pietermaritzburg: University of Kwazulu-Natal, 2006): G. Ruiters, "Black economic empowerment and the South African social formation," pp. 119–26; and U. Duchrow, "Property for people, not for profit," pp. 139–57.
49 See Balibar's discussion of the Hegelian *Rechtsstaat* in *Politics and the Other Scene*, above n. 1, pp. 30–3.
50 *Sidumo and Another* v. *Rustenburg Platinum Mines Ltd and Others* (CCT 85/06) [2007] ZACC 22; [2007] 12 BLLR 1097 (CC); 2008 (2) SA 24 (CC); (2007) 28 ILJ 2405 (CC) (October 5, 2007).
51 *Volks NO* v. *Robinson and Others* (CCT 12/04) [2005] ZACC 2; 2005 (5) BCLR 446 (CC) (February 21, 2005).
52 *Volks NO* v. *Robinson and Others*.
53 *Sidumo*, above n. 50.
54 To warn against the dangers of ideality and idealization is not at all to reject ideals. Cf. Balibar: "Old Marxist, old materialist that I am, I am convinced of this point: the main way of being a materialist, a realist, in politics today is to be 'idealistic' or, more precisely, to raise the question of ideals and the choices to be made between ideals" (Balibar, *Politics and the Other Scene*, above n. 1, pp. 129–45 and 51).
55 Sachs, *The Strange Alchemy of Life and Law*, above n. 8, p. 220.
56 I. Kant, *Critique of the Power of Judgment*, trans. P. Guyer and E. Matthews (Cambridge: Cambridge University Press, 2000), p. 174 (5:294).
57 See Cornell, "Bridging the span toward justice," above n. 2.
58 Sachs, *The Strange Alchemy of Life and Law*, above n. 8, pp. 214–15.
59 Sachs, *The Strange Alchemy of Life and Law*, above n. 8, p. 146.
60 See R. Dworkin, *Law's Empire* (Cambridge, MA: Harvard University Press, 1986).
61 Sachs, *The Strange Alchemy of Life and Law*, above n. 8, pp. 147–8.
62 Sachs, *The Strange Alchemy of Life and Law*, above n. 8, pp. 152–3.
63 Sachs, *The Strange Alchemy of Life and Law*, above n. 8, p. 152.
64 *Matatiele Municipality and Others* v. *President of the Republic of South Africa and Others* (CCT 73/05), decided on February 27, 2006. Albie Sachs, Concurring Opinion.
65 See D. Cornell, *Defending Ideals: War, Democracy, and Political Struggles* (New York: Routledge, 2004).
66 I analyzed this film in D. Cornell, *Clint Eastwood and Issues of American Masculinity* (New York: Fordham University Press, 2009), pp. 151–63.
67 Sachs, *The Strange Alchemy of Life and Law*, above n. 8, p. 183.

Chapter 2

1 I would like to thank the many colleagues and students who have assisted me in developing the arguments in this chapter, in particular Danie Brand (for directing me to the relevant cases), Drucilla Cornell, and Erin Fine.
2 The two different ways to spell judgment/judgement should be noted: I understand the former, judgment, to designate legal decision-making in the strict sense of laying down the law. The latter, judgement, designates a process of evaluation, reflection, weighing, and considering a plurality of perspectives. Sachs's jurisprudence stands for me in the guise of the latter.
3 K. van Marle, "The archaic structures of desire" (2010) *South African Public Law* 25: 195–208.
4 A. Krog, *Begging to be Black* (Cape Town: Random House Struik, 2009).
5 G. Deleuze, *Negotiations 1972–1990,* trans. M. Joughan (New York: Columbia University Press, 1995), p. 173. See also: G. Deleuze and F. Guattari, *A Thousand Plateaus*, trans. B. Massumi (Minneapolis, MN: University of Minnesota Press, 1987); and I. Buchanan and C. Colebrook, *Deleuze and Feminist Theory* (Edinburgh: Edinburgh University Press, 2000).
6 Krog, *Begging to be Black*, above n. 4, p. 95.
7 M. Mamdani, *When Does Reconciliation Turn Into a Denial of Justice?* (Cape Town: HSRC Press, 1998).
8 D. Cornell, *Transformations* (London and New York: Routledge, 1993).
9 C. Douzinas and A. Gearey, *Critical Jurisprudence: The Political Philosophy of Justice* (Oxford and Portland, OR: Hart, 2005), p. 10.
10 Douzinas and Gearey, *Critical Jurisprudence*, above n. 9, p. 10.
11 Douzinas and Gearey, *Critical Jurisprudence*, above n. 9, p. 10.
12 Douzinas and Gearey, *Critical Jurisprudence*, above n. 9, p. 10.
13 Douzinas and Gearey, *Critical Jurisprudence*, above n. 9, p. 3.
14 K. van Marle, "Law's time, particularity and slowness" (2003) *South African Journal on Human Rights* 19: 239–55; "Lives of action, thinking and revolt — a feminist call for politics and becoming in post-apartheid South Africa" (2004) *SA Publiekreg/Public Law* 19: 605–28; "Laughter, refusal, friendship: thoughts on a 'jurisprudence of generosity'" (2007) *Stellenbosch Law Review* 18: 194–206; "Haunting (in)equalities" in R. Hunter (ed.), *Rethinking Equality Projects in Law: Feminist Perspectives* (London: Hart, 2008), pp. 125–46.
15 Van Marle, "Laughter, refusal, friendship", above n. 14.
16 Van Marle, "Laughter, refusal, friendship", above n. 14; and P. Williams, *The Alchemy of Race and Rights: Diary of a Law Professor* (Cambridge, MA: Harvard University Press, 1991).
17 S. Nuttal and A. Mbembe (eds.), *Johannesburg. The Elusive Metropolis* (Durham, NC: Duke University Press, 2008).
18 See Cornell, ch. 1 in this volume. See also É. Balibar, *Politics and the Other Scene*, trans. C. Jones, J. Swenson, and C. Turner (London and New York: Verso, 2002).
19 G. Pavlich, *Governing Paradoxes of Restorative Justice* (London: GlassHouse Press, 2005).
20 R. Bergowitz and D. Cornell, "Parables in revenge and masculinity in *Mystic River*" in D. Cornell, *Clint Eastwood and Issues of American Masculinity* (New York: Fordham University Press, 2009), pp. 121–38.
21 Bergowitz and Cornell, "Parables in revenge", above n. 20, pp. 121–38.
22 M. Foucault, *The Politics of Truth*, ed. S. Lotringer (Los Angeles, CA: Semiotext(e), 2007).

23 S. Woolman, "The South African Constitution as the last modernist project" in S. Woolman and M. Bishop (eds.), *Constitutional Conversations* (Pretoria: University of Pretoria Press, 2008), pp. 25–44.
24 K. van Marle, "Transformative constitutionalism as/& critique" (2009) *Stellenbosch Law Review* 20: 286–301.
25 J. Hyslop, "Gandhi, Mandel, and the African modern" in Nuttal and Mbembe, *Johannesburg*, above n. 17, pp. 119–36.
26 A. Sachs, *The Strange Alchemy of Life and Law* (Oxford: Oxford University Press, 2009), p. 140.
27 Sachs, *Strange Alchemy*, above n. 26, pp. 140–53.
28 Sachs, *Strange Alchemy*, above n. 26, p. 141.
29 Sachs, *Strange Alchemy*, above n. 26, p. 141.
30 Sachs, *Strange Alchemy*, above n. 26, p. 144.
31 Sachs, *Strange Alchemy*, above n. 26, p. 144.
32 Sachs, *Strange Alchemy*, above n. 26, p. 144.
33 H. Arendt, *The Life of the Mind* (New York: Harcourt, 1971), p. 88.
34 See A. Cavarero, *In Spite of Plato: A Feminist Rewriting of Ancient Philosophy* (Cambridge: Polity Press, 1995).
35 W. Smith, "Cosmopolitan citizenship. Virtue, irony and worldliness" (2007) *European Journal of Social Theory* 10: 37–52.
36 Smith, "Cosmopolitan citizenship", above n. 35 44.
37 Smith, "Cosmopolitan citizenship", above n. 35 44.
38 D. Villa, *Arendt and Heidegger: The Fate of the Political* (Princeton, NJ: Princeton University Press, 1996), p. 203; and Smith, "Cosmopolitan citizenship", above n. 35 44.
39 Smith, "Cosmopolitan citizenship", above n. 35 44; and H. Arendt, *Between Past and Future* (New York: Penguin, 1968), p. 225.
40 Smith, "Cosmopolitan citizenship", above n. 35 45.
41 Smith, "Cosmopolitan citizenship", above n. 35 45.
42 *Harksen* v. *Lane NO and Another* 1997 (11) BCLR 1489 (CC).
43 *Harksen*, para. 120.
44 *S* v. *Jordan and Others* 2002 (6) SA 642 (CC).
45 A more problematic observation by them is the following: "By making her sexual services available for hire to strangers in the marketplace, the sex worker empties the sex act of much of its private and intimate character. She is not nurturing relationships or taking life-affirming decisions about birth, marriage or family; she is making money. Although counsel for the appellants was undoubtedly correct in pointing out that this does not strip her of her right to be treated with dignity as a human being and to have respect shown to her as a person, it does place her far away from the inner sanctum of protected privacy rights. We accordingly conclude that her expectations of privacy are relatively attenuated. Although the commercial value of her trade does not eliminate her claims to privacy, it does reduce them in great degree."
46 *National Coalition for Gay and Lesbian Equality* v. *Minister of Justice and Others* 1998 (12) BCLR 1517 (CC).
47 *National Coalition for Gay and Lesbian Equality*, para. 117.
48 *Minister of Home Affairs and Another* v. *Fourie and Another* 2006 (1) SA 542 (CC).
49 J. B. Naude and P. de Vos, "Disturbing heteronormativity: the 'queer' jurisprudence of Albie Sachs" (2010) *Southern African Public Law* 25: 209–34.
50 *Volks* v. *Robinson and Others* 2005 (5) BCLR 446 (CC).
51 *Port-Elizabeth Municipality* v. *Various Occupiers* 2005 (1) SA 217 (CC).
52 *Port-Elizabeth Municipality*, para. 18.

53 *Dikoko* v. *Mokhatla* 2006 (6) SA 235 (CC).
54 *Dikoko* v. *Mokhatla*, para. 105.
55 *Dikoko* v. *Mokhatla*, para. 109.
56 *Minister of Health* v. *New Clicks South Africa (Pty) Ltd* 2006 (2) SA 311 (CC).
57 Williams, *Alchemy of Race and Rights*, above n. 16, pp. 7–8.
58 Williams, *Alchemy of Race and Rights*, above n. 16, p. 8.
59 van Marle, "Laughter, refusal, friendship", above n. 14.
60 Arendt, *The Life of the Mind*, above n.33, p. 88.
61 Woolman, "The South African Constitution", above n. 23, p. 35.
62 Woolman, "The South African Constitution", above n. 23, p. 25.
63 Woolman, "The South African Constitution", above n. 23.
64 Woolman, "The South African Constitution", above n. 23, p. 27.
65 Woolman, "The South African Constitution", above n. 23, p. 31.
66 Woolman, "The South African Constitution", above n. 23.
67 Woolman, "The South African Constitution", above n. 23, p. 28.
68 Woolman, "The South African Constitution", above n. 23, p. 27.
69 Woolman, "The South African Constitution", above n. 23, p. 31.
70 Tshepo Madlingozi's socio-political argument that the law fails to address seriously the needs of the most marginalized and Johan van der Walt's abstract philosophical one concerning law's "sacrificial self-destruction of hospitality," as well as the critique that emanated from the Frankfurt School after the Second World War. Woolman notes that these arguments cannot be totally rejected, but also not admitted in full.
71 Woolman, "The South African Constitution", above n. 23, p. 35.
72 Nutall and Mbembe, *Johannesburg*, above n. 17, p. 1.
73 Sachs, "A gentle provocation: a reply to Stu Woolman" in Woolman and Bishop, *Constitutional Conversations*, above n. 23, p. 37.
74 Sachs, "A gentle provocation", above n. 23.
75 Sachs, "A gentle provocation", above n. 23.
76 Sachs, "A gentle provocation", above n. 23, p. 39.
77 Sachs, "A gentle provocation", above n. 23., p. 40.
78 Sachs, "A gentle provocation", above n. 23.
79 Nutall and Mbembe, *Johannesburg*, above n. 17, p. 1.
80 Nutall and Mbembe, *Johannesburg*, above n. 17.
81 Nutall and Mbembe, *Johannesburg*, above n. 17.
82 Nutall and Mbembe, *Johannesburg*, above n. 17.
83 Nutall and Mbembe, *Johannesburg*, above n. 17., p. 3.
84 van Marle, "Transformative constitutionalism" above n. 24.
85 Nutall and Mbembe, *Johannesburg*, above n. 23, p. 3.
86 2008 (2) SA 24 (CC).
87 2008 (2) SA 24 (CC), para. 155.
88 2008 (2) SA 24 (CC)., para. 55.
89 2008 (2) SA 24 (CC)., para. 51.
90 Nutall and Mbembe, *Johannesburg*, above n. 23, p. 5.
91 Nutall and Mbembe, *Johannesburg*, above n. 17.
92 Nutall and Mbembe, *Johannesburg*, above n. 17, pp. 6–7.
93 Nutall and Mbembe, *Johannesburg*, above n. 17, p. 7.
94 Nutall and Mbembe, *Johannesburg*, above n. 17, p. 8.
95 Nutall and Mbembe, *Johannesburg*, above n. 17.
96 Nutall and Mbembe, *Johannesburg*, above n. 17.
97 Nutall and Mbembe, *Johannesburg*, above n. 17, p. 9.

98 Nutall and Mbembe, *Johannesburg*, above n. 17, p. 11.
99 Nutall and Mbembe, *Johannesburg*, above n. 17, p. 12.
100 Nutall and Mbembe, *Johannesburg*, above n. 17.
101 Nutall and Mbembe, *Johannesburg*, above n. 17.
102 Nutall and Mbembe, *Johannesburg*, above n. 17, pp. 13–14.
103 van Marle, "Transformative constitutionalism", above n. 24, pp. 294–6.
104 Nutall and Mbembe, *Johannesburg*, above n. 17, p. 16.
105 Nutall and Mbembe, *Johannesburg*, above n. 17, p. 17.
106 Nutall and Mbembe, *Johannesburg*, above n. 17.
107 2008 (3) SA 232 (CC).
108 2008 (3) SA 232 (CC)., para. 24.
109 Nutall and Mbembe, *Johannesburg*, above n. 17, p. 21.
110 Nutall and Mbembe, *Johannesburg*, above n. 17, p. 22.
111 Nutall and Mbembe, *Johannesburg*, above n. 17, p. 32.
112 Hyslop, "Gandhi, Mandel, and the African modern", above n. 25, p. 119.
113 Hyslop, "Gandhi, Mandel, and the African modern", above n. 25, p. 136.
114 Hyslop, "Gandhi, Mandel, and the African modern", above n. 25, p. 120.
115 Hyslop, "Gandhi, Mandel, and the African modern", above n. 25, p. 120.
116 Hyslop, "Gandhi, Mandel, and the African modern", above n. 25.
117 Hyslop, "Gandhi, Mandel, and the African modern", above n. 25, p. 122.
118 Hyslop, "Gandhi, Mandel, and the African modern", above n. 25, pp. 122–3.
119 Hyslop, "Gandhi, Mandel, and the African modern", above n. 25, p. 123.
120 Hyslop, "Gandhi, Mandel, and the African modern", above n. 25, p. 124.
121 J. Joyce, *A Portrait of the Artist as a Young Man* (New York: Viking Press, 1964).
122 Hyslop, "Gandhi, Mandel, and the African modern", above n. 25, p. 125. See W. B. Le Roux, "From acropolis to metropolis: the Constitutional Court building and South African street democracy" (2001) *South African Public Law* 16: 139.
123 Hyslop, "Gandhi, Mandel, and the African modern", above n. 25, p. 126.
124 Hyslop, "Gandhi, Mandel, and the African modern", above n. 25, p. 131.
125 Hyslop, "Gandhi, Mandel, and the African modern", above n. 25, p. 135.
126 Hyslop, "Gandhi, Mandel, and the African modern", above n. 25, p. 136. See also H. C. Bosman, *The Collected Works of Herman Charles Bosman*, ed. L. Abraham (Johannesburg: Halfway House, 1994), p. 568.
127 S. Benhabib, *The Reluctant Modernism of Hannah Arendt* (Thousand Oaks, CA: Sage Publications, 1996).
128 Villa, *Arendt and Heidegger*, above n. 38, p. 174.
129 Villa, *Arendt and Heidegger*, above n. 38, p. 174.
130 Benhabib, *The Reluctant Modernism of Hannah Arendt*, above n. 127, p. 22.
131 Benhabib, *The Reluctant Modernism of Hannah Arendt*, above n. 127, p. 27.
132 Benhabib, *The Reluctant Modernism of Hannah Arendt*, above n. 127, p. 28.
133 Benhabib, *The Reluctant Modernism of Hannah Arendt*, above n. 127.
134 Benhabib, *The Reluctant Modernism of Hannah Arendt*, above n. 127.
135 Benhabib, *The Reluctant Modernism of Hannah Arendt*, above n. 127, p. 29.
136 Benhabib, *The Reluctant Modernism of Hannah Arendt*, above n. 127.
137 Benhabib, *The Reluctant Modernism of Hannah Arendt*, above n. 127. See also Villa, *Arendt and Heidegger*, above n. 38.
138 Benhabib, *The Reluctant Modernism of Hannah Arendt*, above n. 127, p. 51.
139 Benhabib, *The Reluctant Modernism of Hannah Arendt*, above n. 127, p. 50.
140 Benhabib, *The Reluctant Modernism of Hannah Arendt*, above n. 127, p. 94.
141 Benhabib, *The Reluctant Modernism of Hannah Arendt*, above n. 127.

142 Benhabib, *The Reluctant Modernism of Hannah Arendt*, above n. 127. Benhabib notes, however, that Arendt in some cases is still influenced also by a view that emphasizes continuity seeking to uncover or recover loss phenomena (p. 95).

143 E. Young-Bruehl, *Why Arendt Matters* (New Haven, CT: Yale University Press, 2006), p. 165.

144 Young-Bruehl, *Why Arendt Matters*, above n. 143.

145 Young-Bruehl, *Why Arendt Matters*, above n. 143, p. 166.

146 Young-Bruehl, *Why Arendt Matters*, above n. 143.

147 Young-Bruehl, *Why Arendt Matters*, above n. 143.

148 Benhabib, *The Reluctant Modernism of Hannah Arendt*, above n. 127, p. 191.

149 Benhabib, *The Reluctant Modernism of Hannah Arendt*, above n. 127, p. 190. See also R. Fine, "Judgment and the reification of the faculties: a reconstructive reading of Arendt's *Life of the Mind*" (2008) *Philosophy & Social Criticism* 34: 155–74; and D. Villa, *Politics, Philosophy, Terror: Essays in the Thought of Hannah Arendt* (Princeton, NJ: Princeton University Press, 1999), pp. 89–90.

150 Nutall and Mbembe, *Johannesburg*, above n. 17, p. 32.

151 My gratitude to Erin Fine who highlighted this after carefully reading an earlier draft of this chapter.

152 Sachs, *Strange Alchemy*, above n. 26, p. 273.

Index

Ackermann, Justice Laurie 4, 10, 42, 85, 89
African National Congress (ANC) 2–4, 5, 6, 7, 10, 11–2, 13–6, 23, 27, 75–6, 78, 79–81, 84, 90–1, 92, 98–9, 100, 111; Freedom Charter of 7, 11, 15, 76, 90–2
Agamben, Giorgio 59
anti-violence 9, 20, 21, 23–4, 75–6, 78, 100
Arendt, Hannah 34, 40–1, 52–5, 59–60, 70–2
armed struggle 1, 3, 6–7, 9, 10, 12–6, 23, 46, 75–8, 100–1
Asmal, Kader 28, 99

Balibar, Étienne 9, 11–2, 15–7, 23, 29, 31, 34, 46, 75–6, 81, 82, 93; civility 9, 11–2, 15–7, 22–5, 43–4, 75, 82–4, 90
Benhabib, Seyla 70–2
Benjamin, Walter 65, 71
Biko, Steven 3
Blanchot, Maurice 59
Bosman, Charles 69

capitalism 7–8, 10–1, 13, 19, 27, 35–6, 37, 64, 70, 71, 93–4, 95
Code of Conduct *see* armed struggle.
Constitution of South Africa 1–2, 4–8, 10–1, 17, 18–9, 20–3, 25, 27–8, 29–35, 37–40, 42, 45–7, 53, 57, 60–1, 68, 69, 73, 85–6, 89, 94–5, 110, 111, 112–3
Constitutional Court of South Africa 1, 5, 11, 16–17, 20–1, 23, 28–9, 31, 36, 42, 44, 56, 63, 67, 77, 84–5, 88, 89, 90, 93–5, 101, 109
constitutionalism 45, 51–3, 62, 65, 66, 85, 104, 109
Cornell, Drucilla 49, 51, 52–3, 73

Deleuze, Gilles 49
Derrida, Jacques 49
Douzinas, Costas 51
Dworkin, Ronald 43

Eastwood, Clint 46, 52

Ferguson, James 63
Foucault, Michel 53
Frente de Libertação de Moçambique (FRELIMO) 1, 87

Hegel, G. W. F. 11, 16–7, 19, 36–8, 81
Heidegger, Martin 71
humanism 52, 53, 55, 56, 57, 61, 68, 69, 73, 85
Hyslop, Jonathan 53–4, 61, 66–9

idealism 1, 6, 19, 38, 43, 46–7, 79–80, 84–6, 112

Joyce, James 67–8
judgment *see* Kant, Immanuel.
jurisprudence 1–2, 5–8, 9–12, 29, 34, 37, 49–60, 61–7, 69–73, 93–5

Kant, Immanuel 36, 38, 40–3, 54, 59, 72, 81, 89, 107, 109
Kelsen, Hans 4, 7, 9–10, 23
Klare, Karl 62, 110
Kotane, Moses 100
Krige, Uys 111
Krog, Antjie 49, 72, 103

Mamdani, Mahmood 51
Mandela, Nelson 2, 7, 53, 61, 66–9, 75–7, 79, 84–5, 86, 107
Marx, Karl 11, 27, 37, 81
Mbembe, Achille 52, 53–4, 61, 62–6, 73
Mokgoro, Justice Yvonne 25–6, 58
More, Mabogo 33
Mureinik, Etienne 95–6, 110

Nedelsky, Jennifer 40–1, 54, 107

O'Regan, Justice Kate 56, 58

Plaatje, Sol 34–5

Rechstaat see Hegel, *G. W. F.*
Revolution: civility and 12–22; ethics and 9, 77, 79, 84–8, 111–2; law and 1–2, 6–8, 84–8, 104–5; procedural (Kelsen) 4, 6, 7, 9; substantive (Kelsen) 2, 4, 5–7, 9–11, 18–20, 23, 38–9, 42, 51–2, 71

Sanders, Mark 100, 104–4
socialism 7, 11, 13, 28, 35–6, 95

Tambo, Oliver 3, 14, 75–6, 77, 78–9, 80, 83, 84, 90–1, 92, 105, 113
Truth and Reconciliation Commission (TRC) 7, 10, 15, 18, 20, 47, 99–101, 103
Tutu, Desmond 79, 101

uBuntu-botho 9, 11–2, 21–7, 31–6, 37, 52–3, 58, 75, 88, 93, 96, 98, 104–7
Unger, Roberto 95

Vasak, Karel 27
Villa, Dana 55, 70

Weber, Max 61, 65, 109
Weil, Simone 52
Williams, Patricia 52, 59
Woolman, Stuart 53–4, 60–1, 68, 69

Yacoob, Justice Zac 29
Young Bruehl, Elisabeth 72